Education's
Highest Aim

Contributors:

Mary Adams, San Antonio, TX
Dennis Cali, Tyler, TX
Chiara Catipon, Los Angeles, CA
Alex Ceolin, Toronto, Ontario
Teresa Ceolin, Toronto, Ontario
Fatima Fajardo, Baltimore, MD
Amarylis Gottt, Loppiano, Italy
Thomas Hartmann, Brooklyn, NY
Mary Hartmann, Brooklyn, NY
Janice Lauer Hutton, West Lafayette, IN
Julia James, Dedham, MA
Maggie James, Dedham, MA
Iola James, Dedham, MA
Ryan Kelley, Oakland, CA
Katie Kelley, Woodstock, IL
Kevin Kelley, Woodstock, IL
Matthew Kelley, Vilseck, Germany
Emery Koenig, Minneapolis, MN
Joseph Koenig, Minneapolis, MN
Karen Koenig, Minneapolis, MN
Katie Krokey, Poughkeepsie, NY
Maria Luca, Toronto, Ontario
Mary McLennon, Chicago, IL
Donald Mitchell, West Lafayette, IN
Merle Mullins, Harrisburg, PA
Katie Mullins, Harrisburg, PA
Lara Mullins, Harrisburg, PA
John Mullins, Harrisburg, PA
Ben Mullins, Harrisburg, PA
Rebecca Mullins, Harrisburg, PA
Molly Mullins, Harrisburg, PA
Sarah Mundell, Rosario, Argentina
Paul O'Hara, Chicago, IL
Judith Povilus, Loppiano, Italy
David Rider, Hyde Park, NY
Steven Rogg, Aurora, IL
Clarissa Rogg, Naperville, IL
Phyllis Rogg, Naperville, IL
Tom Rowley, Houston, TX
Jacklin Saikali, Boston, MA
JP Saikali, Boston, MA
Yvonne Tibbitt, Long Beach Township, NJ
Sharry Tibbitt, Somerset, NJ
Chiara Tibbitt, Somerset, NJ

Education's
Highest Aim

Teaching and Learning
through a Spirituality
of Communion

Michael James, Thomas Masters
Amy Uelmen

Preface by
Anthony J. Cernera

New City Press
Hyde Park, New York

Published in the United States by New City Press
202 Comforter Blvd., Hyde Park, NY 12538
www.newcitypress.com
©2010 New City Press

Cover design by Durva Correia

Scriptural references are taken from the *New Revised Standard Version*
©1989 Division of Christian Education of the National Council of the Churches
of Christ in the United States of America.

Library of Congress Cataloging-in-Publication Data:

James, Michael, Ph. D.
   Education's highest aim : teaching and learning through a spirituality of
communion / Michael James, Thomas Masters, Amy Uelmen ; preface by
Anthony J. Cernera.
      p. cm.
   ISBN 978-1-56548-336-1 (pbk. : alk. paper) 1. Moral education—United States.
2. Education—Aims and objectives—United States. 3. Christian education—
United States. 4. Spirituality—United States. 5. Focolare Movement. I. Masters,
Thomas. II. Uelmen, Amy. III. Title.
   LC311.J35 2010
   370.11'4—dc22   2009051290

Printed in the United States of America

Contents

Preface

*T*he Focolare Movement has been close to my heart for many years. I saw its transforming effect in the life of two dear friends of mine many years ago. The Focolare spirituality of communion gave them the same thing it offers us today — a way of life that allows us to express the gospel in the immediacy of life. I feel both gratitude and a sense of responsibility for the opportunity I had to meet Chiara Lubich and to be part of Sacred Heart University's conferral upon her of a doctorate in Humane Letters. In her acceptance speech, Chiara reminded us of the words of Jesus to his disciples, "May they be one in us, so that the world may believe" (Jn 17:21). She continued by describing the transformative effect that living a spirituality of unity has on others who encounter it:

> If there is unity, the world around us believes. And this is what happened. Many people radically changed their way of life; and others found the strength to respond to God's call or to be faithful to their decision to live for him…. We held everything in common among us, like the first Christian community…. The Movement's communitarian spirituality is based on the law of love, which has the power to transform society…. Thus the spirituality of unity leads humanity to recognize that it is a family. And the living out of this spirituality in society begins to transform its relationships, structures, and laws into those of the family of the children of God, brothers and sisters in Christ. (21 May 1997, Sacred Heart University, Fairfield, CT)

Chiara's call to a communitarian spirituality insists on the importance of our individual responses, because a communitarian life depends upon each of us and the quality of the relationships that we share.

In 2008, the Focolare Movement presented me with the Luminosa Award for Unity, a prize given to recognize persons or groups whose lives and works contribute to the Focolare's goal of universal brotherhood. This honor was another opportunity to rededicate myself to contributing to "that all may be one." On that occasion, I recalled how Chiara and her first companions felt this call to live for unity in the midst of the challenges, difficulties, and devastation of the Second World War. The leaders of our Church and prophetic leaders like Chiara justifiably could have gathered and said, "The world is falling apart. Let's build our bomb shelters and hide in our basements." Or, "Let's build up the walls and protect ourselves from our enemies." Rather, Chiara and her friends chose to affirm a different vision. They were bold enough to imagine the possibility of a world where unity could be achieved. They forged that message not in the best of times but in the worst of times. They announced a message of light and of hope and of the possibility of building God's kingdom when circumstances suggested otherwise. And they began this task by giving themselves completely in service to others, moment by moment. In those early days, guided by the Holy Spirit, they experienced the power of loving as Jesus loved, expecting nothing in return. In essence, they experienced the reality that we are most fully ourselves when we are in communion with God who is Love.

The task of becoming human is a lifelong project. We are not born complete. Education at every level must be devoted to contributing something meaningful to this task of becoming fully human. As president of a Catholic university, I feel fortunate to be part of a tradition whose wisdom asserts that the education of the person is the education of the *whole* person. Ideally, Catholic educators and their collaborators accept the responsibility of fostering genuine community, of creating environments that demand cooperation and mutual support, of providing opportunities for students to be served and in turn serve those in need, and of teaching the process of critical reflection on the prevailing cultural values that potentially enhance or damage human living.

In its characteristic way of discovering and building upon points of unity, the Focolare Movement has now produced this text that demonstrates the universality of these educational goals. *Education's Highest Aim* grounds its witness in the twin premises that the self is most fully defined as "a moral self" and that the self can, therefore, only move toward integrity within the realm of community. The personal stories come from teachers, students, parents, administrators and scholars who are committed to education's highest aim. Further, the cases come from diverse educational settings in public schools, private schools, Catholic schools, home schools, and universities throughout North America, the Caribbean, and Mexico. The authors make no direct claims that *these* stories encompass the totality of educational issues or hold the key to educational success, yet I come away from each case with a sense that I, too, could apply the underlying principles of each experience in my own day-to-day educational environment. In typical Focolare fashion, the simplicity of the gospel message — to love one another — comes through in the experiences of these diverse respondents who have one thing in common — their desire to put the gospel into practice.

I am convinced that the work and the charism of the Focolare Movement is critically important if we are going to create the kind of world where we can live together as human beings who are made in the image and likeness of God and who have dignity and worth because we are loved unconditionally by God. The reality of unity is such that one must participate in it in order to achieve it. And, while each of the protagonists in these narratives demonstrates distinct choices made in unique contexts, in some way the formation of persons as an integrated whole is at the center of each story. The spirituality of unity succeeds at this process of formation in an extraordinary way.

We can participate with them if we only create the kinds of opportunities that the Focolare Movement creates all the time. This spirituality of unity brings people together. And, in the bringing together and in the experiencing of life and of sharing with each other, sometimes new things happen beyond our imagination and a greater unity is achieved. We need to keep inviting one another to *participate*. The way to create this greater unity is to invite people to participate in the creation of that unity.

Here is an educational philosophy, a pedagogy and a practice grounded in the vision of unity, in a spirituality of communion. It is one that invites students, faculty, staff, administrators and families to work cooperatively for the development of the whole person into his and her best self in service to the common good. This is an educational aim of the highest order worth working together to achieve.

Anthony J. Cernera, Ph.D.
President, Sacred Heart University, Fairfield, CT,
and President of the International Federation
of Catholic Universities

Introduction

$\mathcal{A}$merican education has its problems, to be sure. Parents want their children to develop the skills, knowledge, and maturity needed to live and work in an age of expanding opportunities and challenges and shrinking social, economic, and geographical boundaries. Students want to do good work, but find the content, routine and pace of school excruciating compared to the swift, complex rhythm of the other aspects of their lives. Teachers have to satisfy multiple and equally important roles — maintaining order; inculcating culture and values; transmitting information; developing and executing effective strategies that meet both short- and long-range objectives; facilitating students' construction of personality, relationships, and knowledge; keeping and reporting detailed, accurate records; establishing and maintaining collegial relationships with peers and with supervisors; balancing students' need for autonomy with parents' need for feedback; translating policy to practice; satisfying the public's demand for accountability; forestalling burnout by renewing themselves intellectually, professionally, spiritually. School administrators have to maintain the tradition that the public expects, while simultaneously renewing and transforming them to meet ever-changing and ever-expanding mandates. Policy makers, whether public or private, have to balance their limited resources against the boundless needs of educational systems.

In a pragmatic society like that of the United States it is tempting to construe such problems as occasions for finding solutions. Once they are "fixed," the problems will go away, leaving us free to do more important and satisfying things. Like all temptations, such a strategy leads not to resolution but to larger and more complex problems. Instead, the extensive experience of parents, students, teachers and administrators who have sought to live out a spirituality of communion reveals how such problems present opportunities for ongoing reflection and action that lead not to solutions but to engagement and renewal. This book presents an analysis of the state of contemporary education in the light of a way of life rooted in love of neighbor, and the consequences of living out such a value in the many educational milieus.

What Does This Book Contain?

Education's Highest Aim includes four chapters:

- "Re-imagining Education through a Spirituality of Communion" outlines the principal tensions in the world of education, particularly between the ideal and the actual, and between relationship and individuality. It then discusses how they can be re-imagined through a spirituality of communion. It presents strategies for negotiating constraints on the construction of moral identity; locates this study within the context of other inquiries into the intersection of faith-based perspectives and professional life; presents its methodology and evidence; and outlines the fundamental educational tensions that will be addressed through narratives.

- "The Focolare Movement and Education: Background and Sources" presents the context from which the protagonists in the narratives (presented in Chapter 3) operate. It presents the story of the origins of the Focolare Movement and its engagement with culture in general and educational culture in particular through the formation of young people, its ongoing academic reflection in the Abba School, and its involvement in various educational milieus through "Education and Unity" and the various schools, including the Sophia University Institute, which have emerged from students and scholars living out a spirituality of communion.

- "Theory and Practice: Applying a Spirituality of Communion in Academic Settings" contains twelve narratives that document the consequences when individuals or small groups, known as "living action cells," have lived out a spirituality of communion. The experiences come from the perspective of students, teachers, parents, and school administrators, whenever possible using their own words. These narratives include a gamut of contexts, including private and public elementary, middle, and high schools; home schools; and universities.

- "Appendix of Primary Sources" contains five texts by the founder of the Focolare Movement, Chiara Lubich. They reveal both the mystical and practical dimensions of a spirituality of communion as it is lived out in the context of education.

Who Could Profit From This Book?

This book is intended for anyone who has a stake in education — parents and other family members; students, school personnel, teachers, and administrators at every level; educational researchers; school board members; legislators and other policy-makers. *Education's Highest Aim* presents the theoretically coherent and practically effective way in which hundreds of people from across the United States, the Caribbean, Canada, and Mexico have negotiated the problematic realities inherent in education. Anyone interested in education achieving its fundamental goals could profit from reading and discussing *Education's Highest Aim*.

How Can This Book Be Used?

We have designed this book so that a variety of readers might put it to various uses:

- The narratives in Chapter 3 can be read for their own sake as compelling and, at times, moving stories.

- Those who have an interest in the Focolare Movement will find a narrative history of how its spirituality of communion has spread throughout the Movement itself, and throughout North America. The narratives illustrate how a wide range of people in the most varied settings have put its principles into effect. The appendix contains a thematic collection of primary sources by the Focolare founder, Chiara Lubich.

- Groups such as Parent-Teacher Associations, home-schooling collaboratives, or book discussion forums can use *Education's Highest Aim* as a springboard to an examination of how and why schools can be effective, and what might be done to help bring about such success.

- Those in positions of school leadership will find an effective institutional model that can be used as a basis for reflection and planning.

- In-service teachers can use *Education's Highest Aim* for personal reflection on their vocation as educators, as well as for discussion with their peers about how to deal with realities they must face every day in their classrooms, departments, and schools.

- University professors of education and their classes can use *Education's Highest Aim* to examine effective theory and praxis, grounded in a historical context.

- Researchers will find a model that begins with a clear theoretical statement, contextualized in history and validated through narrative analysis, organized into thematic narratives. This method of investigation could be applied to a variety of other educational situations.

All readers, however, should keep in mind that at its heart this inquiry, as well as the theory and practice that it outlines, is profoundly spiritual. Education, a fundamentally humanistic endeavor, succeeds to the extent that it recognizes the moral identity of all those involved in it, an identity that springs from the essence of human beings created in the image and likeness of a God who is love. This realization takes on certain dimensions for Christians, but the "Art of Loving" that underlies so many of the stories in *Education's Highest Aim* is not solely Christian. It is deeply divine, but at the same time deeply human. Like the Golden Rule, it is a code that all people of good will can follow on their way to better relationships and better social structures.

It is our hope that *Education's Highest Aim*, in a small but significant way, contributes to fulfilling the summons to which Chiara Lubich directed her life in response, a summons to the highest and best for every human being: "That all may be one."

1

Re-imagining Education through a Spirituality of Communion

𝒯he driving idea behind *Education's Highest Aim* is that it is possible to step back from the perceived dichotomy between theory and practice in order to imagine the educational endeavor in a new way. It starts from the framework of a spirituality of communion as developed and lived out within the social and cultural context of the Focolare Movement. Those who follow this new way of participating in the educational enterprise approach their experience through a spirituality whose goal is the fulfillment of the last prayer of Jesus Christ before his death, "that they may all be one" (Jn 17:21). What does such a lofty and what might seem an exclusively theological goal have to do with education? Focolare founder Chiara Lubich explains:

> The goal that has always been assigned to education (to form the human person, so as to render him or her independent) is implemented, almost paradoxically, by forming the person-in-relationship, which for us means the human person in the image of the Trinity, one who is capable of continually transcending self.... It is through this spiritual and educational practice of mutual love, to the point of becoming completely one — a practice followed by all the members of the Movement, since all are called to live this communitarian experience in small groups — that we work toward the achievement of the goal of all goals, expressed in Jesus' prayer and testament: "May they all be one." (*Essential Writings* 223–24)

Lubich suggests that there are "two goals of education: to teach the individual and to build the community" (*Essential Writings* 223). For over sixty years, students, parents, teachers, professors, and administrators who have constructed their personal and professional lives on a gospel-based spirituality of communion have discovered that it is possible to live for both goals simultaneously. Their experiences embody not so much an answer to the problems they encounter within the educational system and milieu but a way of living within the inherent tensions and transforming the reality around them.

> In our approach ... in which the spiritual and the human penetrate one another and become one ... [e]ducation's goal, its highest aim, becomes a reality.... [W]e experience the fullness of God's life, which Jesus has given us, a trinitarian relationship, the most genuine form of social relationship, in which a wonderful synthesis is achieved between the two goals of education: to teach the individual and to build the community. (*Essential Writings* 223)

Educational Practice, Theory and Identity Formation

The list of complaints about American school systems is familiar. According to some, in comparison with their peers in other parts of the world, students from the United States seem to study less and therefore to know less as a consequence of their time in school. In many contexts, the lack of discipline in the classroom and in the school as a whole makes for an uncomfortable or even dangerous experience for students and teachers alike. For a variety of reasons, many parents have not prepared their children for the school experience and do not take an active role. Some even relate to schools as child care centers rather than as places at which they can work together with school personnel to help their children grow. It is commonly believed that the brightest young people are not attracted to pursuing education as a career and that many of those who are competent, facing the tension and frustration of the school environment, soon leave the teaching profession. Even where educational research has identified the most effective practices for teaching and learning, institutional inertia coupled with the drive for accountability forces schools to focus not on the most effective practices but on test preparation, thus blocking the hope for systematic change.

It also must be noted that there are many "schools that work." Stories of student achievement (both cognitive and affective), of reform initiatives by inspirational teachers and administrators such as those in Ted Sizer's Coalition of Essential Schools; in models such as Cristo Rey, NativityMiguel, KIPP, or many other charter school designs; or in the many projects inspired by the thought and technique of Paulo Freire demonstrate the resilience and creativity of people in every area of education.

Education's Highest Aim does not intend to probe the truth or falsity of these criticisms and claims. Nor does it summarize or analyze the literature that puts forth proposed solutions. Rather, it explores some of the deeper tensions that these problems may reflect, namely those between the ideal and the actual, between relationship and individuality, between the common good and isolation.

FUNDAMENTAL TENSIONS IN EDUCATION THEORY AND PRACTICE

The tensions named above weave their way through the philosophical foundations and historical movements of American educational policy and practice. On the one hand, an ideal for education in a democratic society points toward open-ended and collaborative pedagogical approaches and expected outcomes. For example, John Dewey, the modern father of experiential education, suggests that in order to foster students' capacity to contribute to society, educators and educational policy must be rooted in five premises:

- The distinctive worth and capacity of every person;
- The importance of educating each person to become significantly engaged in contexts of social action and experience;

- The centrality, both for learning and democracy, of each student's direct and collaborative involvement with core issues and challenges in the making of democratic community;

- The belief that in democracy, as in science, the combination of multiple and different understandings makes progress attainable;

- The insistence that this kind of learning is a lifelong endeavor and commitment, not a matter for schools alone. (Orrill 330)

Dewey's aim, then, was a form of learning directly suited to building democracy as a participatory, moral, and justice-seeking framework for lives lived in common.

On the other hand, the overriding operative educational philosophy in contemporary American society generates an intensely individualized model of learning. In "Education for a World Lived in Common with Others," Lee Knefelkamp and Carol Schneider describe this mode of education practice as

> ... centered in and on the experience, interests, and unique understanding of the independent learner. As such, this conception fundamentally parts company with the dialogical, interactive foundations of the Deweyan vision of learning. In place of cooperative problem-solving and orientation toward social action and moral democracy, this individualized conception of learning leaves experiences of social connection and communal obligation essentially on the periphery. (Orill 333)

Within this framework, the ideal of an educational philosophy such as Dewey's that gives priority to democratic relationships often founders on the twin shoals of entrenched individualism, discernibly at the core of American culture, and the weight of institutional inertia.

It can be argued, then, that educational philosophy is trapped within a dilemma. Schools would like to improve, but the realities of social, cultural and familial contexts seem to pose insurmountable obstacles. Many educators, parents, students and policy makers who seek to explore more democratic and collaborative possibilities lose direction in a social and cultural context that essentially revolves around the individual.

NEGOTIATING THE TENSION BETWEEN THE INDIVIDUAL PERSON AND PERSONS IN RELATIONSHIP

If one of education's goals is to teach the individual, it is important to consider what, for the purpose of this book, we mean by "the individual." For Chiara Lubich and for the respondents whose narratives are contained here, the individuals are most themselves when they recognize and accept God's love for them (see 1 Jn 3:1), and for each person they encounter. This existential means of defining the self implies two things: the possibility of a completely integrated self (given that each person exists first and foremost as a child of God) and the necessity that identity be defined authentically in terms of relationship to the other. For someone who tries to live the Focolare's spirituality of communion, the goal of "teaching the individual" really becomes one of "teaching individuals how to recognize God-Love within themselves and within each other person." And the twin goal of "building the community" becomes, to a certain extent, both the method and the consequence of individuals who are discovering God-Love. The choices of individuals in response to their community (i.e., the relationships that come about) will either damage the community or build it. And the identity of those individuals becomes defined by these choices. This framework suggests that if we are educating individuals *and* attempting to build community, we must be about the work of forming individuals who are integrated within themselves — individuals whose identity does not change from one situation to the next. This framework comfortably equates "identity" with "moral identity," because it begins from the belief that persons fulfill their identity only through the experience of reciprocity. Citing Gandhi's maxim, "You and I are but one. I cannot injure you without harming myself," Lubich comments:

This means knowing how to "make yourself one" with others, that is, making your own their burdens, their thoughts, their sufferings, their joys....

Certainly, for those who set out to move today's mountains of hatred and violence, the task is gigantic and overwhelming. But what is impossible for millions of isolated and separate individuals becomes possible for people who have made mutual love and mutual understanding the center of their lives. (*Essential Writings* 14)

Through reciprocity with others, individuals realize their capacity to confront the weightiest moral questions, life's "mountains of hatred and violence" that no one can move by himself or herself, and in doing so become most truly themselves. In the contemporary world of education, the construction of such an integrated identity in its constituents (students, parents, instructors) is complicated or thwarted by tensions such as these:

- Professionalization and specialization lead to academic success and recognition but impose a work ethic based on isolation that deters teachers and researchers from developing reciprocal relationships;

- Privileged contemporary notions such as competency and efficiency require persons to display only fragments of their talents, characteristics, knowledge, and experience so as to fulfill the technical requirements of the particular educational setting in which they must operate;

- Students and educators alike adopt sets of behaviors that maximize their reward and minimize their personal cost;

- The processes that constitute much of the day-to-day educational activity, such as problem-solving or decision-making, render human subjects solitary agents who apply their calculative or manipulative capacities in an instrumental fashion;

- Educational institutions seek to be good stewards of public as well as private resources but often choose to reduce themselves to a commodity with the central promise of economic success and social rewards for the individual student.

Education's Highest Aim explores these tensions in the context of a theory of moral identity, with the intent to inspire constructive action. The individuals represented in this book who seek to implement the Focolare spirituality have discovered a means of overcoming potentially demoralizing tensions. They hold in common the idea that the consequence of an approach to education informed by a spirituality of communion is rooted in a deeper understanding of each participant's moral identity. The narratives in Chapter 3 make a case for the construction of moral identity within students, teachers, administrators and families in the modern educational milieu through reciprocal and caring relationships, even while operating within the problematic realities described above. In educational settings marked by isolation, fragmentation, discontinuity and individualism, these protagonists have generated counter-currents of interdependence, relational action, dialogue, and reciprocity.

EXISTENTIAL IDENTITY

Two contemporary philosophers have contributed in a particular way to our thinking about moral identity formation and to that of many other educators: Charles Taylor and Alasdair MacIntyre. They outline two compelling characteristics of moral identity. Taylor explains the notion of the self and identity as characteristically relational — in other words, we come to understand self, society, and the world not through our individual actions but through dialogue within ourselves and with others. MacIntyre maintains that the full expression of a virtue in someone's life is intelligible only as a characteristic of a unity of life, a life conceived and evaluated as a whole.

These two concepts — first, that the fundamental notion of self-identity has to be conceived of as being-in-relationship, and second, that moral identity is meaningful only when an individual has a personal understanding of his or her internal essential unity — are further explored within a spirituality of communion. Chiara Lubich's phrase "existential identity" affirms both of these ideas. For Lubich, existential identity "overcome[s] the fracturing and fragmentation that people often experience in relation to themselves, to others, to society, to God, while at the same time drawing out the originality, the unrepeatable uniqueness of each person" (*Essential Writings* 221).

She describes existential identity as the intent to achieve unity with another through a process of emptying oneself to be fully present to the other, with the goal of achieving reciprocal love. She explains, "My identity cannot be achieved either by being defensive or by opposing others, but only through communion" (*Essential Writings* 265).

Another perspective is proposed by Margaret Urban Walker, who maintains that relationships have meaning and are understood only in terms of how they are constituted among particular persons (166). In other words, we cannot understand the relationship between two individuals without understanding the context of their relationship. Carol Gilligan, in her *In a Different Voice,* describes the distinctive sorts of understanding related to this particular way of understanding as "contextual and narrative" rather than "formal and abstract." The latter "abstracts the moral problem from the interpersonal situation," whereas the former invokes a "narrative of relationships that extends over time." Both Walker and Gilligan would say that true understanding of relationship requires two elements: the context and concreteness of individuals (with their specific history, identity, and affective-emotional constitution) and the special context of history, identity, and affective definition that constitute a relationship. Practically, for Walker, this means that

> [I]ndividual embroideries and idiosyncrasies, as well as the learned codes of expression and response built up in particular relationships, and built up culturally around kinds of relationships, require of us acute attention to the minute and specific, to history and incident, in grasping cases in a morally adequate way.

If the others I need to understand really are actual others in a particular case at hand, and not repeatable instances or replaceable occupants of a general status, they will require of me an understanding of their/our story and its concrete detail. (167)

Only with this understanding, Walker claims, can a person respond with authentic care and concern and so enter fully into the experience of the other.

The theoretical foundations for moral identity and discourse that Taylor, MacIntyre, Walker and Gilligan each describes must be recognized, understood, and rooted in experience and practice. Lubich would add, "Precisely because of this existential unity between word and life, between saying and doing, many people have found [the Focolare] experience credible and convincing." Lubich observes in her own life that "this experience provokes profound changes in people on an existential level, thereby setting in motion true educational process" (*Essential Writings* 221).

FRAGMENTATION, SELF AND SECULARISM

Education's Highest Aim offers descriptive narratives to examine how a spirituality of communion might contribute to the conversation about educational philosophy and practice centered around three themes related to the formation of an existential identity:

- beyond fragmentation: the unity of a life
- beyond the self: unity with others
- beyond secularism: a communitarian spirituality

Beyond Fragmentation: *Education's Highest Aim* focuses on understanding moral identity within the educational culture rather than on analyzing professional roles. A role is what we do. Studying the role of a scholar, teacher, or student would result in a list of attributes, behaviors, expectations, and responsibilities organized typologically and used to predict or explain behavior. In "The Dialogical Self" Charles Taylor develops the notion of how moral identity is linked not *merely* to what we do but to "who" we are. The question of who I am can be answered by describing my profession: "I am a musician"; or by stating my function: "I am an administrator at X university"; or sometimes by stating a relationship, "I am X's spouse." In this way I tell who I am by situating myself in some sort of professional, social, or familial category. But the kind of identity crucial to having a coherent sense of self must relate to a broader ethical space. To have identity is to know "where you're coming from" when it comes to questions of value or issues of importance. Moral identity defines the background against which individual persons know where they stand on such matters. To have that called into question, or to fall into uncertainty, is not to know how to react. Consequently, they cease to know who they are in this ultimately relevant sense.

Beyond the Self: In this context identity must be explored not in terms of the self defined by a set of distinct roles, obligations, and behaviors but in terms of unity of the self. MacIntyre describes a unified self and explains why the concept is difficult to grasp:

> [A]ny contemporary attempt to envisage each human life as a whole, as a unity, whose character provides the virtues with an adequate telos encounters two different kinds of obstacles, one social and one philosophical. The social obstacles derive from the way that modernity partitions each human life into a variety of segments, each with its own norms and modes of behavior. So work is divided from leisure, private life from public, the corporate from the personal. And all these separations have been achieved so that it is the distinctiveness of each and not the unity of the life of the individual who passes through those parts in terms of which we are taught to think and to feel. (204)

MacIntyre's social obstacle, then, consists in life being construed as a series of unconnected episodes, leaving individuals unable to conceive of a life in terms of what he calls "virtues." Those who genuinely possess virtues can exhibit them in many different types of situations, even those in which social norms do not expect virtue to have any meaning.

He explains the philosophical obstacles to understanding the self as a unity of a life in terms of

> ... two distinct tendencies, one chiefly, though not only, domesticated in analytical philosophy and one at home in both sociological theory and existentialism. The former is the tendency to think atomistically about human action and to analyze complex actions and transactions in terms of simple components. Hence the recurrence in more than one context of the notion of "a basic action." (204)

Assuming that particular actions derive their character as parts of larger wholes is a point of view alien to the dominant ways of thinking in modern society, yet one which must be considered if life is to be understood as more than a sequence of independent actions and episodes. In a similar fashion, existentialism makes a sharp separation between individuals and the roles that they enact, rendering life nothing but a series of unconnected episodes.

Beyond Secularism: An overview of the literature on faith and the professions, sociological studies of work, and research on the academic profession suggests two competing visions of the world. The first is a secularization thesis — informed by the Enlightenment — that holds, among other notions about the individual and society, that an inherent characteristic of progress in a pluralistic society is an increasingly clear separation of traditional religious institutions and culture from public life. Consequently, there exists an historical resistance to spiritually-based conversations about education. In *Educating for Life*, Thomas Groome suggests that American culture imposes a subtle but clear expectation upon educators that their work must transcend the influence of their own spirituality, thus precluding a prime source of humanizing influence. Groome argues that "Without spiritual foundations, educators are left with only philosophical ones, and although the latter are necessary and valuable, they are neither 'innocent' by way of objectivity nor 'sufficient to the task.'" He continues, "Ironically, American education has drawn most heavily, almost exclusively, from one school of philosophy — pragmatism — and yet has been phobic about its spiritual neutrality" (16).

Narrative As an Interpretive Methodology

A framework for exploring moral identity at the intersection of faith culture and modern educational culture could be conceived in several different ways. An empirical approach would consider the professional and religious dimensions of a group as a source of values to be identified and then correlated with individual behaviors. This is the approach that most social science research has employed in the study of religion and the academic profession. The results of such an inquiry would emerge in the format of a statistical analysis. An alternate framework would ground an examination of the professional and religious dimensions in an Aristotelian conception of the practical. This is the approach taken by many scholars of ethics in studies of professions, social systems and institutions. Such an examination would be presented through descriptive and normative theory. A third framework would ground an examination of the professional and religious dimensions in character or virtue ethics. This kind of examination is best revealed through narrative.

In "Constancy and Forgiveness: The Novel as a School for Virtue," Stanley Hauerwas suggests that narratives offer not theoretical explanation, but involvement in a way of life. The narrative process employed in *Education's Highest Aim* facilitates a coherent examination of a "way of life" or the "self." This process goes beyond the mere description or telling found in biography or autobiography. It is a journey with profound consequences for the narrator. It instigates a process of reflection that leads narrator and reader alike to new ways of self-understanding and uncovers values and customs previously taken for granted. Hauerwas asserts, "Theory is meant to help you know the world without changing the world yourself; a story is meant to help you deal with the world by changing it through yourself" (15).

Education's Highest Aim uses narrative as the primary vehicle for what Clifford Geertz calls a "thick description" of how stakeholders in education construct their identity at the intersection of academic and religious cultures, with emphasis on the tensions they negotiate at specific moments in their experience. We recognize, as Taylor explains, that "self-descriptions include moral or ethical self-characterizations, that is, descriptions that situate us relative to some goods, or standards of excellence, or obligations that we cannot just repudiate" (305). Acknowledging that ethos and identity inform each other, *Education's Highest Aim* explains how these particular individuals find meaning as participants in education. This approach offers something new because very little sociological research attends to the educational profession with a substantive consideration into the meaning of spiritual ethos and educational practice.

The particular narratives we analyze are grounded in an overarching narrative, the experience of the Focolare Movement. Such "self descriptions" are analyzed to reveal how existential identity is formed within multiple and competing ethical contexts, how it is that individuals deal with the world by changing it through themselves, and how they assess themselves and their various component parts in relation to standards informed by the prevailing educational culture and by a culture animated by a particular spiritual wisdom.

These tensions are identified as dynamic moments within each individual's story — lived experiences that might yield a deeper understanding about ethos and practice. In other words, it is anticipated that the way that we live might be illuminated through the choices that must be made in the face of a dilemma. Previous studies of the world of education generally have overlooked such tensions. *Education's Highest Aim* investigates the way that people with particular faith commitments — in this case, parents, students, teachers, and administrators — live their lives. This study, then, is an account of the world of education as it is lived, embodied, and expressed in an ethos, a way of life for individuals in a variety of educational settings — and how that ethos is embodied in their identities.

Education's Highest Aim suggests that educational problems might be addressed by looking beyond the relatively technical, pragmatic, and tactical responses often relied upon to eliminate the difficulty in a given situation. In contrast, narrative interpretation allows questions of educational ethics to be considered as dilemmas that must be faced rather than problems that must be solved, an approach that in ethical matters poses deeper challenges that no specific policy, strategy, or behavior can resolve. A narrative methodology of ethical analysis makes it clear that such persistent problems require behavior that sensitively, decorously, and appropriately fits the enduring challenge. *Education's Highest Aim* approaches problems like a mystery rather than a puzzle, asserting that most of the deeper moral demands in life require not technical responses but fitting rituals.

READING THE NARRATIVES

In the "Narratives" section (Chapter 3), stakeholders in primary, elementary, middle, secondary, homeschool and university settings relate their own attempts to make a positive impact on their environment and as a result maintain a unity of self. These narratives are presented in terms of the particular moral dilemmas readily found in academic settings, and are analyzed to reveal how such "problems" have been negotiated through a spirituality of communion. These problematic situations include:

- Working to establish dialogue in situations where individuals tend to be isolated because of existing traditions, practices and structures;

- Maintaining personal values in circumstances when they seem outweighed by social, professional, and possibly economic rewards of academic success;

- Decentering traditional authority structures in classrooms and in institutions without sacrificing order and discipline;

- Embracing and transforming the tension produced when individuals who understand their identity as being essentially relational confront the ethos of autonomy that suffuses American society;

- Identifying and redressing prejudgment that prevents authentic, reciprocal relationships (between students, between students and faculty, between faculty);

- Transforming perfunctory responsibilities or duties into opportunities for reciprocal relationship;

- Articulating an authentic identity within constraints such as age, race, or gender;

- Empowering learners whose individual differences impede their establishment of reciprocal relationships and their full participation in education;

- Transforming the common practices of institution-based norms that may not value the person over efficiency, productivity, and control.

In her 2000 address at The Catholic University of America, Lubich describes the importance of unity — the essence of a spirituality of communion — in the fragmented reality of contemporary education:

Unity is a very timely aspiration. Despite the countless tensions present in our world today, the entire planet, almost paradoxically, is striving toward unity. Unity is a sign and a need of our times. However, this drive toward unity within people — as the etymology of the word "education" (Latin *e-ducere:* "draw forth") indicates — must be drawn out in a positive way. This implies, on all levels of human endeavor, an educative process consistent with the demands of unity, so that our world will not become a Babel without a soul, but an experience of Emmaus, of God with us, capable of embracing the whole of humanity. This might seem a utopia. But every authentic educational approach includes a utopian thrust, that is, a guiding principle that stimulates people to build together a world which is not yet a reality, but ought to be. In this perspective, education can be viewed as a means for drawing nearer to this utopian goal. (*Essential Writings* 222–23)

With this in mind, in each narrative the nature of a problem is discussed, then the experience of particular individuals or groups who attempt to establish a coherent existential identity through dialogic and reciprocal relationships is related. Such experiences offer templates for negotiating within complex academic contexts by suggesting reasonable and rational ways of engaging such tensions. The experiences presented in *Education's Highest Aim* reveal an "authentic educational approach" in action, and offer a glimpse of the utopian goal that this book presents for serious consideration to students, to parents, to practitioners, to scholars, and to policy makers.

These experiences have a common denominator: their protagonists were seeking to live out a spirituality of communion, which they came to understand and appreciate through one of the ecclesial movements, the Focolare. Chapter 2 presents a brief account of the Focolare's origins and its initiatives that relate to the world of education.

2

The Focolare Movement and Education: Background and Sources

"*So* what do you do?" It is a common question to those involved in one of the relatively new ecclesial movements such as the Focolare Movement. Many groups and projects within the Church have wonderfully concrete answers to this question: we pick up dying people off of the streets, we help women dealing with crisis pregnancies, we run soup kitchens or homeless shelters. We can see and touch how these actions help to fix a particular problem.

What does the Focolare Movement do? What does it fix? There are answers, but it might take an additional step to see and touch them. The Focolare does sponsor several social projects throughout the globe, some of which are large and well-developed. But these projects do not in and of themselves capture the heart of what people in the Focolare Movement are "doing."

In order to fully understand what the Focolare "does" requires a broader sense of what it means to contribute to building up the life of the Church and of society. Its spirituality of communion embraces not only the more concrete dimensions of service, but also the more interior work of allowing the life of the gospel to permeate our ordinary lives and our work in the culture as a whole. Through this wider lens, what becomes clear is that a movement such as the Focolare originates not in a plan for social action, but as a response of the Holy Spirit to the critical challenges we face in this millennium.

In this chapter, we offer some background information that might illuminate both the context in which the contributors to this volume are working and the sources to which they refer. It begins with a brief sketch of the origins of the Focolare Movement, then touches on some of the dimensions of the Focolare's work, which have informed its approach to education such as youth formation programs, and structures for reflection on how the Focolare spirituality might inform one's daily work or academic discipline. It concludes with a brief overview of some of the specific institutional structures most directly related to the Focolare's work in education, which have emerged over time: schools and, most recently, a graduate degree program.

ORIGINS

Considering the focal point for this collection of reflections, education, one could draw an immediate connection between the Focolare Movement and education: the founder, Chiara Lubich, was by training an elementary school teacher with an avowed passion for philosophy. While it would be fascinating to study further the connections between Lubich's early teaching experience and the Movement that emerged, that would barely scratch the surface of the deeper story.

Lubich's studies and teaching career were both interrupted by the drama of World War II, as her hometown in northern Italy, Trent, became a strategic target for heavy bombing. Amidst the disastrous ruins of the war, as all of their dreams for the future were crumbling before their eyes, Lubich and her friends discovered that God is the only Ideal that never dies, that God is love, and that the life of the gospel put into practice could be the solution to every personal and social problem. Since several of their homes had been destroyed, they gathered in a small apartment that came to be known as the "Focolare" (which in Italian means "hearth") because of the warm atmosphere of family and love that continues to be characteristic of these communities.

As the war continued to rage, they frequently met in the bomb shelters, with a small book of the gospels in hand.

Conscious that any moment could be their last, they asked themselves what might be the words especially dear to Jesus. They discovered, "This is my commandment, that you love one another as I have loved you" (Jn 15:12), and they understood the measure of his love: he gave his life. Lubich remembers how they gathered in a circle and made a pact: "I am ready to give my life for you; I for you; each one for the other." The effort to keep the flame of mutual love alive among them became their lifestyle.

In another moment, as they took refuge from the bombings in a dark cellar, they opened the gospel and read by candlelight the solemn page of Jesus' prayer before dying: "I ask not only on behalf of these, but also on behalf of those who will believe in me through their word, that they may all be one. As you, Father, are in me and I am in you, may they also be in us, so that the world may believe that you have sent me" (Jn 17:20–21). Lubich described that moment: "It was not an easy text to start with, but one by one those words seemed to come to life, giving us the conviction that we were born for that page of the gospel" (*Essential Writings* 4). The commitment to building unity remained their decisive focus. As Lubich remembered, "One thing was clear in our hearts: what God wanted for us was unity. We live for the sole aim of being one with him, one with each other, and one with everyone. This marvelous vocation linked us to heaven and immersed us in the one human family. What purpose in life could be greater?" (*Essential Writings* 17).

Within a short time, a community that included people of all different age groups and vocations — families, children, priests, men and women of various religious orders — began to take shape. When the war ended, people of the community who traveled to other cities for work or study carried with them their newly discovered lifestyle. Focolare houses were opened first in other cities in Italy, then throughout Europe and, starting in the late 1950s and into the 1960s, in North and South America, Asia and Africa.

The early origins of the Movement also provide a powerful nucleus of ideas for its emerging vision of the renewal of culture and social life. At a certain point in her own philosophy studies, Lubich was struck by this thought: "You are inconsistent because you are searching for the truth in philosophy while every morning you are in communion with the one who is truth: Jesus." This, she explained, gave her the push "to put my beloved books in the attic, in order to follow him" (Fondi, 466–68).

When the books eventually came down from the attic, they were received into a community focused on the constant renewal of mutual love in all of its relationships, so as to receive the gift of unity and to experience the presence of "Jesus in their midst" (see Mt 18:20) as the one to illuminate their studies and what that implied for culture. In a passage she wrote in 1949, Lubich poetically draws out the connections between the spiritual life and the transformation of culture: "We need to allow God to be reborn within us and keep him alive. We need to make him overflow onto others like torrents of Life and resurrect the dead. And keep him alive among us by loving one another.... So everything is renewed: politics and art, school and religion, private life and entertainment. Everything" (*Essential Writings* 316).

What impact would this have on the lives of the ordinary people who make up the Focolare Movement? Over time, within the Movement there emerged several kinds of vehicles for communal reflection on what it might mean to live a spirituality of communion in one's daily life, and for mutual support in working through the inevitable challenges and obstacles that one might encounter. Most relevant to the topic of education are the structures that serve formation of children and youth; those that support sustained reflection on work in the field of education; and finally, those that support scholars in their effort to draw out the implications of the spirituality for theoretical reflection.

BUILDING A NEW SOCIETY TOGETHER

The Focolare reached an important juncture in 1956. In response to the brutal repression of the Hungarian uprising, Lubich launched an appeal: "There is a need for authentic disciples of Jesus, not only in convents, but also in the world. Disciples who follow him voluntarily. An army of voluntary people, because love is free, capable of building a new society ... that gives testimony to one name: God."[1]

People from the most various social backgrounds and areas of professional life took on this commitment to live a spirituality of communion in their personal lives, with their families, and in their work lives. They gather together frequently to encourage one another and work through the inevitable challenges that this calling entails. "New Humanity" is their vehicle for outreach and for collaboration with all those committed to renewing society. We can highlight just two aspects of their approach: first, where two or more committed to living the Focolare spirituality are in the same work place, they create a "living action cell," in which through their constant commitment to live mutual love, they strive to let Christ's living presence among them illuminate all of their relationships, their approach to their work, and also how they face particular problems, in order to be a vehicle for building unity in that particular environment.

Second, they come together according to "worlds" — not sliced out according to their particular tasks or professional specializations, but as people committed to building unity in a particular sector of social or professional life. For example, a gathering for the "world" of health care could include reflections and responses not only from doctors and nurses, but also from aides, therapists, hospital janitors and patients — all committed to building relationships of love and unity in the context of a hospital. Similarly, a gathering for the "world" of education could bring together administrators, students, teachers, counselors, coaches and maintenance staff. This approach serves not only to break down the artificial barriers among the various roles in social life, but also to help each participant to embrace the unified whole of a given environment.

Several of the contributors to this volume have been applying the Focolare spirituality to their own work in the field of education and reflecting on this effort together with others who share a similar commitment. Some have also had the opportunity to experience how a "living action cell" of mutual

---

1. See http://www.focolare.org/page.php?codcat1=294&lingua=en&titolo=social%2 0aspects&tipo=social%aspects(31 August 2009).

love lived together with others can transform a specific educational environment. Finally, many have brought the fruits of their efforts to the events for cross-disciplinary reflection that has in turn opened their horizons to how people in other roles and serving other tasks experience that particular environment. This capacity to embrace the "whole" of a given educational context provides an especially rich and textured basis for reflection.

YOUTH FORMATION

In the mid-1960s, the youth branches of the Focolare Movement began to take shape. In the various Focolare communities which at that point already dotted the globe, young people of various ages, in college, high school, and elementary school, began to gather in small groups to repeat, in essence, the initial experience of the group of young women in Trent. On the basis of a "pact" to love one another, Focolare youth meet regularly to share their joys and difficulties in living out a spirituality of communion and then reach out to build relationships of love and unity with the youth around them.

Their program of formation includes basic instruction in the truths of the faith and moral life, including support for their efforts, as they put it, to "go against the current" of a culture permeated by consumerism, hedonism and egoism. They work to keep God at the center of their lives and to foster a spirit of genuine love and service to others as a consequence of this choice. Their classmates and friends are often touched by the joyful witness that emerges from their lifestyle. The Church is already seeing the consequences of this younger generation's commitment. Three Focolare youth who died in their late teens or early twenties are on the path to canonization, already proclaimed as Servants of God.

International congresses and gatherings which in recent years have coincided with the "World Youth Days" help them to open their hearts to the universal dimensions of the family of the Church, and to assume responsibility for the work of building a world of peace, justice and solidarity. The "credo" on the current website of "Youth for a United World," their vehicle for outreach to young people throughout the world, indicates the kind of formation that the Focolare spirituality fosters:

> We believe it is possible to build a better world, one with greater solidarity, and to create one human family where the identity of each person is respected. We use every available means to foster unity, to heal the existing disunities in this worldwide family: among generations; between groups and movements; among Christians of varied denominations; between believers of different religions. We want to tear down the barriers that divide ethnic groups, races, peoples, cultures, social classes, people of different convictions and persuasions.[2]

Within the breadth of this vision of living for a united world, the youth who participate in Focolare activities and formation programs are encouraged to see love as the heart of every aspect of their life, and so to discover in their own everyday lives "a wonderful unity." As Lubich explained, their "lives would not be dull and flat since they would not be made up of bits juxtaposed and disconnected (with the time for lunch, for example, having nothing to do with the moment for prayer, and with mission set aside only for a specific hour, and so on)" (*A New Way* 77). In contrast, by living the spirituality of unity one discovers how every aspect of life — even the most concrete and mundane — can be rooted in and be an expression of love.

Against this backdrop, they discover that studies, too, can be lived as an aspect of love. Lubich stated that we study "Because we love God. When you love someone, when you fall in love, you want to know everything about the other person" (*A New Way* 158). Further, every kind of knowledge can be at the service of love.

Several contributors to this volume are familiar with the Focolare's programs for youth formation, either through their own experience of growing up in the Movement, or through their active involvement as adults assisting in the formation of children and youth. Thus their contributions are grounded

---

2. See http://www.mondounito.net/spip.php?article3&lang=en.

not only in reflection on specific writings that draw out the implications of the spirituality of communion for the field of education, but also from their own experience of this spirituality's impact on their lives and the lives of the young people with whom they are in contact.

What happens when academics live a spirituality of communion? Since January 1991, the Focolare's interdisciplinary study center, familiarly known as the "Abba School," has met regularly to probe the spiritual legacy of the Movement in light of Christian doctrine and tradition, and to explore the novelty that it offers for the cultural challenges of our times. The group includes university professors, lecturers, and researchers representing various specializations in theology, philosophy, and the social and natural sciences.

Each meeting begins with the "pact" of being ready to give their lives, one for the other, if not physically at least spiritually and intellectually. Concretely, this requires a readiness to "let go" of one's own way of thinking in order to try to enter into the thought of the other. For example, an expert in Thomism "lets go" of this expertise in order to "enter into" the thought of another, perhaps an expert in Bonaventure, or in another school of thought. From this communion emerge intuitions that become "truth" for everyone. The same method is applied not only within the various theological currents, but also among all the different disciplines represented, among experts of different Christian churches, and in comparisons with the affirmations of the great religions (Fondi, 471). As theologian David Schindler summarized in his introduction to an English translation of a recent collection of essays from the study center, this method "testifies to how we must resist assuming that the response needed to the problems of our time can be realized easily or quickly — for example, through management techniques or political strategies or 'expert' analyses." Rather, Schindler surmises, the study center embodies a much more promising method, "namely, a reflection sustained by and centered in a life of community and entailing a transformation of one's being and consciousness through prayer, the suffering of difference, and the like, all of which presuppose the duration of time" (*Introduction to the Abba School* 14).

Beyond this relatively small group of professors, through periodic gatherings the experience of the Abba School is extended to other college and university professors working to thread out the implications of a spirituality of communion for various fields of academic research. Some of these gatherings emphasize the inter-disciplinary conversation; others provide space for more specific reflection and critique among scholars of the same discipline. The contributors to this volume who have participated in these gatherings have found their own academic reflection formed and informed by both the inter-disciplinary and discipline-specific Abba School gatherings.

"EDU — Education and Unity"[3]

It is not surprising that within a Movement dedicated to building unity, vehicles have developed to bring together the practical experiences of those working in the various fields and the theoretical aspects of reflection within the parameters of a given discipline. For example, the Focolare's project for renewing economic life draws together not only the practical observations of those running and working in the businesses that emerged in response to Lubich's seed ideas for an "Economy of Communion," but also the theoretical implications of the model that professors and students of economics, business and management theory are exploring.

The international education project entitled "EDU — Education in Unity," still in the initial stages of its development, holds great promise. Its first international convention, "The Community as Educator," held in April 2006, welcomed 500 scholars and educators from 31 countries. Participants explored the viability of a pedagogical approach that places primary concern on caring for all the relationships in the educational process.

---

3. The EDU website can be accessed at http://www.eduforunity.org/. It is in Italian, but some of the studies to which it links are in English.

A galvanizing force for forming this space for reflection began with the conferral on Lubich of honorary doctorates from universities throughout the world that recognized the implications of a spirituality of communion for the most varied fields of culture. A degree in social sciences from the University of Lublin in 1995 was followed by twelve others, including degrees in theology, communication, philosophy, economics, and psychology. In 2000, Lubich received an honorary degree in education from The Catholic University of America in Washington, D.C. Her formal discourse on that occasion, as well as more informal exchanges with professors and students during her visit to the university, have become foundational texts for all who are working to draw out this spirituality's implications for the field of education.[4]

INSTITUTIONAL MODELS

The latest buds to bloom on the tree that has grown from the seed of Lubich's spirituality are various institutional models that demonstrate its creative dynamism. Since the 1990s, in some countries pre-schools and elementary schools have been opened in response to specific and often dire educational needs. These projects serve as laboratories to study not only how a spirituality of communion might inform an institutional structure, but also how it fosters economic and social development. The limited space in this volume allows us to explore only two, Colegio Santa María, in Puebla, Mexico; and the Café con Leche School in Santo Domingo, the Dominican Republic.

Most recently the Movement has taken its first steps in creating institutional models for university education. A prototype, the "Summer School for a Culture of Unity," began in August 2001, in Switzerland. A group of 50 university and graduate students pursuing degrees in a range of disciplines participated in a two-week course for four consecutive summers. Eventually the program drew a total of 250 students from 36 countries and every continent. The interdisciplinary

---

4. See "The Charism of Unity and Education," pp. 129–135.

program worked to foster in each student and each professor a profound synthesis of faith, culture and life.

The summer school served as a creative testing ground that enabled the Movement in October 2008 to open the Sophia University Institute located in the Focolare community of Loppiano, near Florence, Italy. Having already received approval from the Vatican Congregation for Catholic Education to be constituted as a pontifical university, Sophia now offers a two-year interdisciplinary master's degree in "Foundations and Perspectives of a Culture of Unity," and a corresponding doctorate.

As with the summer program, in every aspect of the Sophia curriculum, exploration and discussion of theory are deeply connected to the commitment to practice, which in turn is understood in the context of the renewal of authentic relationships in a concrete life of community. The program is also enriched by daily practices that nourish in each participant the commitment to keep what is termed "mutual welcoming and acceptance" as the point of reference for every aspect of the program.

The brief syntheses of the institutional models included in this volume are intended to serve only as an appetizer. Much more could be said about how these projects might shed light on paths to renewal for other educational institutions.

CONCLUSION

So what does the Focolare "do"? Might it be said that the Focolare "does" culture? Yes, but this could also be somewhat reductive. Perhaps the best way to capture the heart of what the Focolare "does" is with the text by Lubich cited earlier: "We need to allow God to be reborn within us and keep him alive. We need to make him overflow onto others like torrents of Life and resurrect the dead. And keep him alive among us by loving one another."

The Focolare's primary goal is to help ordinary people, from all different backgrounds, in the course of their everyday lives, to make contact with the life of God, and to nourish the continued growth and development of this life by fostering relationships of mutual love. This enables them to receive the gift of unity, God's own presence on earth, which can then permeate and transform every aspect of human life, from the personal to the public, from the religious to the secular.

For Focolare people in the "world" of education, be they students, parents, teachers, administrators, development officers, secretaries, janitors, librarians, scholars or textbook editors, their reflections on their work are grounded in this central experience of the transformative power of love and unity, because in this light, "... everything is renewed: politics and art, school and religion, private life and entertainment. Everything."

3

Theory and Practice:
Applying a Spirituality of Communion in
Academic Settings

INTRODUCTION

These narratives are based upon the experience of
people whose lives have been influenced by the spirituality of the Focolare Movement. The Focolare, one of the "new
ecclesial movements" that have emerged within the Roman
Catholic Church, counts among those who follow its spirituality Catholics, Christians of many other denominations, Jews,
Muslims, followers of world religions, and people of goodwill
who profess no particular system of belief. It is devoted to
unity, specifically to fulfilling what Jesus Christ prayed shortly
before his death: "Father, may they all be one" (Jn 17:11).

The Focolare has been active in North America since 1959
and in that time has led thousands of people from all walks of
life to build unity in their particular circumstances. A central
practice in the Focolare is living out what is called "The Word
of Life," that is, finding practical ways to apply in the many
circumstances of daily life a single verse of the gospel. In local
communities, individuals share their experience of doing so.
Witnessing to the possibility of positive action through the
narration of such experiences has always been an important
part of the culture of the Focolare communitarian spirituality.

In preparing this study, we sent out a "call for experiences"
to individuals or groups who had been living the spirituality
in educational settings throughout the United States, Canada,
and the Caribbean. We received nearly a hundred, reflecting
the diverse milieus in which those who follow the Focolare

live and work. A careful reading and analysis of these narratives brought into focus how individuals or small groups have negotiated fundamental tensions having to do with unity of life and unity with others. For the twelve narratives in this chapter, we have selected experiences that reflect a range of participants (students of various ages, parents, teachers, administrators), of settings (primary, elementary, middle, secondary, home, and university), and of interpersonal and institutional tensions.

Although the protagonists in these narratives often experience a sense of fulfillment, these narratives do not present formulaic "success stories" of how to solve education's many problems. Instead, they offer templates for constructive action in the problematic situations that inevitably arise. To respect the privacy of the individual persons and institutions in these narratives, pseudonyms have been substituted for their proper names. "Strengthening the Identity of Religiously Affiliated Institutions in a Pluralistic Environment," which has been published previously in another form, includes actual names, as does "Establishing Educational Institutions through a Spirituality of Communion."

Like any community, the Focolare has its own lexicon. Terms whose meaning might not be readily apparent include:

- "The Ideal": Chiara Lubich and her early companions in the Focolare spoke of "living for an ideal." "The Ideal" signifies the ideal of unity at the heart of its charism, as well as the way of life of the Focolare taken as a whole.

- The "Art of Loving": a rubric by which a gospel-based way of life is spelled out in specific behaviors. Those of other convictions, religious or secular, have adapted the Art of Loving to their particular moral or ethical systems. Chiara Lubich offers a complete explanation in "Children, Springtime of the Family and of Society," pp. 138–144 in the appendix.

- "The Cube of Love": a game-like activity in which different statements from the Art of Loving are applied to the six sides of a die. This also is explained in

"Children, Springtime of the Family and of Society," pp. 138–144 in the appendix.

- "The Word of Life": a short biblical phrase, selected each month for the entire Focolare Movement worldwide, used as a basis for reflection and action by those who live the Focolare spirituality.

- "Living the present moment": maintaining focus on the essential value of each individual experience by not dwelling on the past or being distracted by anxiety about the future.

- "Jesus in the midst": a reference to Mt 18:20, "For where two or three are gathered in my name, I am there among them." One of Chiara Lubich's early insights was the significance of this passage, in which Jesus Christ promises his actual presence among believers who acknowledge him. This lies at the heart of social action in the Focolare spirituality, because when individuals act together in his name, it is Jesus himself who acts.

- "Make yourself one": describes the effacement of self necessary in order to leave a relationship open to the presence of Jesus in the midst. In "The Beginnings," pages 3–11 in *Essential Writings*, Chiara Lubich explains her understanding of this phrase, as well as other scriptural passages that lie at the heart of a spirituality of communion.

- "Jesus Forsaken": a reference to Mt 27:46, "My God, my God, why have you forsaken me?" another key insight in a spirituality of communion. At this moment, when Jesus Christ felt abandoned even by his Father, he lost everything, taking upon himself the totality of negative human experience. For those who live the Focolare spirituality, this moment when Jesus suffered most is also the moment he loved most, demonstrating the value of suffering when it enters a person's experience. Rather than something to be avoided, it becomes something to be embraced, because it is a presence of Jesus himself and an opportunity to love. See "The Beginnings," pages 3–11 in *Essential Writings*, for a succinct explanation of Jesus Forsaken.

Enhancing Reciprocity in a School Environment

Teachers and students who want to create a reciprocal classroom experience through dialogue run up against the "individualized conception of learning" (see page 20) described by Knefelkamp and Schneider. Those who seek to establish a less individualistic, more collaborative environment in their classrooms and schools have to contend with the unseen heavy hand of habits, conventions and structures. Sometimes, things can be shaken up merely by trying something new. Experienced students, teachers, administrators, and parents know, however, that it takes more than mere novelty to effect meaningful change. Real and effective educational transformation originates from individuals' fulfilling their moral identity and establishing genuinely reciprocal relationships.

Those in the Focolare Movement who work with young people found that school aged children responded well to a technique based upon gospel values, the "Cube of Love." The engaging, game-like quality of this technique helped children in Focolare youth groups put the essential tenets of the gospel into practice. Teachers and students who lived a spirituality of communion found that the Cube of Love provided an effective, engaging way to extend the essence of their experience into educational environments, both religious and secular.

This Cube is premised on what Lubich has called the "Art of Loving," that is, an ethos of reciprocal human interaction such as that contained in the Golden Rule. Each side of a six-sided die is labeled with a component of the "Art of Loving": "Love everyone," "Be the first to love," "Love Jesus in the other," "Share the other's hurt or joy," "Love your enemy," "We love one another." At a given moment, often at the beginning of the school day, the class will roll the Cube and take the result as their watchword. At another moment, often at the end of the day, students and teachers share their experiences. In secular schools, this technique has been adapted in various ways, such as a "Cube of Peace," on which the six sides read "I'm the first to love," "We love one another," "I forgive the other," "I listen to the other," "I love the other," and "I love everyone." Teachers at one Toronto school developed a "Math + Virtues Cube," which pairs mathematical symbols with particular pro-social values. When their students roll this Cube, their possibilities include "+ ADD more love, bring PEACE to everyone"; "- TAKE AWAY suffering, be CHARITABLE"; "x MULTIPLY your love, have COURAGE"; "= LOVE EQUALS a more united world"; "% 100% of the time, FORGIVE" or "÷ DIVIDE with others, show JUSTICE."

Using the Cube of Love has helped schools establish a consistent ethos, transforming their cultures from ones based on rules to ones based on relationships. This changed way of being translates not only into interpersonal relationships, but into extracurricular activities and academic performance. Nancy McNair, a first-grade teacher in a multi-ethnic Chicago classroom, found that even students who at first scorned the activity found themselves participating within a few weeks. She cites changes in their casual conversation that indicate acknowledgement of reciprocity:

"I can be the first to love. Here, you can borrow my red crayon."

"You hurt me but I forgive you. Do you want to play ball with us?"

"Do you want to help me do this puzzle?"

A five-year-old in Norma Monaco's Toronto classroom said, "I know who my enemy is.... It is M, who doesn't want to share with me." A sixth-grade student at her school, one who himself has a reputation among his peers as a bully, wrote this experience of personal change through the Cube of Love:

The other day a student in Grade 8 bullied me after school. He kept pushing me. I told him to stop several times, and I got very upset, but I knew it wasn't right to fight. I thought about the Cube of Love and how I should love my enemy, so I just walked away. That night I prayed that God would forgive this student.

In her inner-city Baltimore classroom, Basima Gabayan begins each day by having her first-graders sit in a circle on the floor and they take turns rolling the Cube. She notes, "Their favorite thoughts are 'Be the first to love' and 'Love your enemy.' " She is moved by the way they help each other live the thought suggested by the Cube; by their willingness to make up immediately if they have disagreement; and by hearing them say to one another, "That's not loving," or "Why don't you just say sorry," or "That's not the right way to treat your brother or sister." She offers this vignette as an example of the effect of the Cube on the behavior of students who previously lacked the social skills to negotiate conflict with their classmates:

> One of my difficult students had an argument with another classmate. I had to pull him out of the classroom and talk to him. I was amazed to hear him say, "I'm sorry Ms. Gabayan for not making the right choice."
>
> When he came back in the classroom, it took him a few minutes to make the first move. He was struggling. First he pretended to be absorbed by swinging in between desks. Finally, he found the courage to approach the other classmate and say, "I'm sorry for hitting you." He then shook his classmate's hand and gave him a hug.

Frank Singer, who runs a private tap dance studio in upstate New York, uses the Cube as a way of extending the scope of his instruction beyond the physical requirements of dance. He has found that it has helped the students become sensitive to one another's needs, especially those who are struggling. He reflects, "The students are learning how to love, their parents are impressed with the changes they see in their children, and my goal of teaching more than tap has been realized." One fourteen-year-old student summed up the effect of the Cube in a note to Singer: "There have been so many weekends when

50

I leave your studio knowing that I've learned something about tap, but more importantly about life."

In her Chicago classroom, McNair found her own demeanor and pedagogy changing: "I found myself responding to their [her students'] love by spending more time listening to their ideas and suggestions. I tried to incorporate their ideas into my lesson planning, which enhanced the lessons and made learning more fun." Monaco also observed a gradual change in her classroom, and in her students' families:

> As the months went by, I could feel that there was always more harmony because the children were trying to love more each day. I could sense a family-like atmosphere among us. I even had parents commenting on the change that they saw in their children and how pleased they were that the school was not only looking after their child's academic needs but building good character traits as well.

One of McNair's colleagues observed similar changes: "Rolling the Cube of Love and discussing the ways we are going to love during the day has created unity, a sense of belonging, enhanced self-esteem, patience and caring for everyone in the classroom."

Using the Cube of Love also contributed to improving academic performance. McNair's school adopted a new science curriculum that required cooperative learning. Instead of the two weeks which the program suggested for training the students, only two days' practice was needed, leaving more time for the actual study of science. On the school's Terra Nova standardized test, she notes, "Scores improved dramatically, perhaps because the students worked so well together and stayed on task."

The teacher who supervises intramural sports at Monaco's school in Toronto was skeptical about its applicability. "I thought that the Cube of Love could work in many forms but not in sports. From my experience, sports was 'Win at all costs ... better to die trying on the sport field than dying by not trying at all ... death, before dishonor ... take no prisoners.' And here, I was asked to do a Cube of Love 'GENTLE' intramurals." The results exceeded his expectations:

The players from different grades definitely had different athletic abilities. I noticed a smaller, younger player going through all the players and taking a shot and scoring. A clean path had opened up for him! When I asked why the other team members let him do that, one of the better players said, "Sir, he has to score too!" I was taken aback.

This teacher then reflected on the global effects of the Cube on his students' lives:

The greatest effect of something is to see its values being practiced long after the lesson has been taught. The children continued to practice the Cube of Love principles in the schoolyard long after the intramurals had finished. The idea of the better players including those with lesser abilities playing together, and the whole notion that we can make everyone feel better, feel welcomed, feel wanted, feel loved, that's how the Cube of Love came alive for me. I went from being a skeptic to a believer!

The Cube of Love has spread to other schools in Toronto. Monaco notes that in 2007 the assistant to the Minister of Education, having heard about the various projects based on it, stated that she could see theory being put into practice. These children, she declared, formed as they were by their experience with the Cube, would be the builders of a more harmonious and peaceful society.

Wilma Unger, who has over thirty years' experience teaching kindergarten through high school in New Jersey, summarizes the Cube of Love's value in activating the latent reciprocity in school environments and its effect on education as a whole:

Ultimately, the greatest contribution to education is that this program addresses conflict resolution and violence that so often accompany our children to the classroom. In the amazingly diverse society we share today, a school can create a new "culture" based upon sensitivity and respect for one another. Then not only will the students have learned the greatest lesson of all (to love as Jesus taught us), but all the other lessons presented to them throughout the day can now take place in an atmosphere conducive to optimum learning.

The ethos of individualism and autonomy that suffuses schools in the United States produces a paradoxical tension. Acting as an independent and free agent can also compel teachers to assume a solitary role, detached from the essential being-in-relation that makes school life enriching and productive. Living out a spirituality of communion in a school setting allows school personnel to identify what may be lacking in their experience and invent strategies for working productively within that tension.

Steve Thomas, with over twenty years' experience in the classroom, is one of four fourth grade teachers at a public school in Houston, Texas. He describes his situation there in these terms:

> My colleagues at that grade level worked pretty much autonomously and independent of the others. Although we all got along very well each teacher had her own territory and ways that weren't to be changed. Challenged by the gifts of the spirituality of communion I never felt completely peaceful about this arrangement. I was constantly looking for ways to bring us together to build more of a team.

He had to work against traditional roles and functions, even against school architecture, which confines their actual work to teachers' individual self-contained classrooms. He sought to break down such limits by greeting his colleagues one by one each day, offering them his help, and inviting them into his classroom to hear his students present their science projects. At a certain point, he recounted "I even began to pop my head into each room and greet the teachers."

This last tactic provoked an opening. "As I walked down the hall one of the teachers shouted after me. With a fairly loud voice she said, 'Stop! Are you always this joyful? I want to know what you are taking to be this happy, and I want to know right now!'" That demand allowed him to share his personal story, in particular his desire to face the seeming randomness and meaninglessness of experience by living for an ideal, as Chiara Lubich and her first companions, inspired by the gospel, began to do during the bombardments of Trent during World War II. He invited her to join him in a practice that members of the Focolare community call the "Word of Life," in which they consider a particular phrase of scripture for a month, and gather weekly to share experiences of putting it into practice in their shared context.

Thomas' intention of bringing his colleagues together into a team — to release the tension of working individually through reciprocity — began to come to life. First with the one teacher, then with three others and a secretary, he began to meet weekly to build community and to share experiences. The group's diverse religious backgrounds reinforced their sense of community. One of the group noted, "This is amazing! Who would have imagined a Baptist, an Episcopal, two Catholics and a Methodist sitting around a table sharing how they live the gospel?"

Linda Johnson's experience parallels Thomas'. She has worked for twelve years as a registered nurse at a New York City preschool for emotionally disturbed and learning disabled children, two to five years old. At the beginning of her career there, her supervisor would ask her to complete clerical tasks. She considered such requests inappropriate. "I thought to myself," she writes, "I am a professional nurse. I could be doing more important things." Such thoughts made her feel uneasy, however. She notes, "I was putting my being a nurse ahead of my being a Christian. I had to start over, 'to be' love. That's what matters!"

Her supervisor, noticing her willingness to build an atmosphere of reciprocity, began to rely on her to mediate conflict among the staff. "Working with professionals is not always easy. Our egos get in the way of building relationships," Johnson writes. At the school, sixteen clinicians having to share nine offices had led to turf wars and arguments. Because of her position as a nurse, she was able to build relationships with all of the staff by answering their health-related questions or dispensing advice. Eventually, the staff resolved their problem together through more careful scheduling; Johnson explains, "Space is always limited, but love is not."

Thomas also shared an example of how the group's solidarity affected the milieu of his Houston school as a whole. A complaint to the principal by some of the teachers concerning the quality of work performed by the janitor roiled the atmosphere among all of the staff and became an issue taken up by members of the Word of Life group.

> The Word of Life for that month was, "Love your enemy." The teachers wanted to do something about this but were at a loss as to what would be effective and yet loving. I suggested that we try an approach that would be somewhat indirect. I suggested that we act like "little sponges," and every time we heard a negative comment about the custodian we should not make matters worse. We should absorb the comment and return it with a positive about him. For example, a complaint would be returned with, "Yes, but did you know he helped two children with their homework yesterday?" The same would happen if he had a complaint about any of the teachers. Although this experience went on for several months, the end result was the teachers and the custodian having lunch together at the conclusion of the year and going into the summer break feeling much better about one another.

Thomas' group succeeded in generating an alternative narrative to the one that would compel both teachers and custodian into their usual solitary roles. Certainly the experience brought about a kind of bonhomie among the staff that made the school a more pleasant place to work; but even more significantly, they allowed the teachers and the custodian to satisfy for each other the powerful human need for community and reciprocity.

At Johnson's school a core group of twelve also formed, including the director, the business manager, the admissions director, two occupational therapists, a psychologist, a teacher, two social workers, a secretary, and a bookkeeper. This "living action cell" (see page 37) includes Christians, Jews, and Muslims. This diverse group shares two things — their proximity to one another as they work in the same school, and the desire to live a spirituality of communion.

At one point, two members of this group — the director and Johnson — evaluated the school to ascertain whether it was the opportune moment to create an interdisciplinary team model based on the "unity" approach, whereby dialogue among members could be facilitated and in turn the team could reach conclusions through discussions based on mutual respect and understanding. They felt that they could best explain the meaning of a "unity" approach by allowing school personnel to experience it first hand. To do so they invited each department in for listening sessions, where members could speak freely to the director, who in turn could get to know them better and discover each group's strengths, weaknesses and conflicts.

At a staff development day a month later, Johnson and the director provided feedback on these sessions, generating open, honest dialogue about the positive and negative dynamics in the school. The two elaborated a "unity" approach to conflict resolution, a five-point process:

1. Take the initiative to reach out to all co-workers and be open to those who reach out to you;

2. When something happens that causes disunity, do not take things personally, try to think positively and forgive if necessary, and take the first opportunity to reach out to the other;

3. Encourage team members with expertise relevant to the discussion at hand to express their thoughts freely, especially taking care to elicit comments from those who are least likely to express their ideas;

4. Try to listen fully before responding or speaking;

5. Resolutions and conclusions from interdisciplinary discussions should be made in the best interest of the students and families we serve and agreed upon by the team.

As a consequence, according to Johnson, the "staff was truly joyful and united at the end of the day. The process of change had begun."

The experiences of Thomas and Johnson illustrate how being-in-relation means that the other, distinct from self, contributes to and evinces what is potentially in the self, awakening school personnel to that which they are capable of being.

GENERATING COMMUNION AMONG TEACHERS

The dynamics of age, race, and gender can lead teachers to adopt an identity that masks their authentic self, leading to turf wars and isolation. They stake out their own space, but such independence comes at a cost — the support and sense of unity that come from reciprocal relationships. If not made with sufficient sensitivity to complex and subtle personal and social currents, gestures intended to generate reciprocity sometimes bring about the opposite effect. This is what happened between John Hansen and a newly hired fourth grade teacher at his Houston public grade school. At the beginning of the school year, he greeted her and let her know that if she ever needed help she could call on him. She was young and African-American, beginning at a school where all of the other teachers were white. Instead of welcoming his gesture, she seemed to have considered that accepting his offer to collaborate would signal weakness, or perhaps hierarchical subservience. He regretted the failure of what he intended as a welcome and continued to seek other opportunities to break through the professional isolation with which she had chosen to shield herself.

Halfway through the school year an opportunity to bridge the divide presented itself. His arms full of books and papers, Hansen was following her to the entrance when she slipped through and let the door slam in his face. In the time it took for him to set down his things, take out a key, and open the door, she had walked around the corner to her classroom and begun a conversation with another teacher. Hansen overheard her saying, "I just don't know what to do. Martin Luther King's holiday is coming up, and I want to do something to raise awareness of this great man." As his class was preparing a play about King, he asked if she could help them. She immediately brightened up and accepted his offer. Later she would reveal that she had been trying unsuccessfully to make a lesson plan that she thought would work and that his invitation gave her a way of accomplishing what she considered an important educational objective. As Hansen narrates the incident, "In the next thirty minutes she was in my room no less than five times to offer further suggestions for the play. The play went very well, with the local press covering the event. A picture was published in the paper with the two of us hugging on the stage."

The new teacher sought competence, dignity, and effectiveness. Because of his commitment to live a spirituality of communion in his workplace, Hansen wanted to enter into a reciprocal relationship that would provide both of them the opportunity to serve their students well. Hansen's initial offer of help made him appear to be seeking a position of power, an unintended effect of his direct approach that forestalled the collaboration he sought. Paradoxically, the opportunity to share not his strength but his weakness provided the opening for both to enter into a relationship of interdependence that allowed something greater than the mere sum of the two to emerge.

GENERATING COMMUNION BETWEEN TEACHER AND STUDENT

Pre-judgments on the part of any of the participants in an educational transaction can force them into roles or particular sets of behaviors that seem to minimize the possibility of conflict, but in practice lock them into a dynamic that limits them as teachers or students, as well as limiting them as human beings. The resolution to such a lack of continuity in personal identity through living out a spirituality of communion in an educational context can be illustrated with an experience by

Eugene Schneider, a professor of English at an urban university on the East Coast.

At the beginning of one semester of freshman composition, Schneider was upset by the affect and behavior of one student, whom he calls "Robert." From the very first day of class, his gruff tone of voice, his defensive body language, and his unblinking stare conveyed his discomfort at being in the classroom. And Schneider, who liked to establish a one-to-one contact with each of his students, felt that "Robert was spreading a dark gloom over the whole left side of the room."

This impasse was surmounted through Schneider's act of solidarity with a different student's problematic behavior during a class discussion.

> At one point a real big guy in the last row raised his hand and then started telling us what he was thinking about the topic. He was not sure about what he wanted to say, however, and kept drifting. I wanted to encourage him and the others to open up, so I tried to make myself one with him and wait for him to say something I could pick up on and connect with our discussion. But he kept circling around it and then started rambling and saying some silly things.
>
> Two students in the front row started to giggle and elbow each other, so I felt I had to love the big guy even more and all the way to the end. I stepped from behind my desk and stood right between the two giggling students and leaned forward, directing my interest intensely toward the guy in the back. When the students saw how serious I was and so focused on what the guy was saying, they too turned and listened. I was praying all the while that the big guy would say something I could build upon. Finally, he managed to come up with a sentence that was somewhat related to the argument we were working on and I cut him off with, "Now there's an important idea that we should all think more about as we write our next paper!" At that point the bell rang and the students filed out.

The "big guy" acknowledged Schneider's attempt to save his dignity with a sigh of relief as he left, but it was Robert, whose resistant actions had poisoned the classroom atmosphere, who called out, "Hey, wait a minute! Please wait! I have to tell you something."

In the office, Robert explained that he had responded as he did to Schneider because of the teacher's physical resemblance to a hated high school teacher whose class he had left with great relief. Robert explained, "But then today when I saw you step between those giggling students and listen with such respect to that big guy rambling all over the map, I saw that you were different. Very different. And I'm sorry I thought you were mean like him." As he was leaving Robert said: "I think I'm too cynical about people. I really have to change. I just had to talk to you. I just had to thank you."

It is interesting to note that what allowed Robert to shed his mistrust was not something that Schneider said or did directly to him, but a positive act on behalf of another in order to allow that student to escape an uncomfortable situation he had constructed for himself, and to retain his dignity. As Schneider notes, "In trying to love the guy in front of me, to make myself one with him, I was giving a strong witness to that boy over by the wall that I was not aware of."

Robert had adopted a particular student role of resistance in order to avoid a perceived cost to his dignity and self-esteem. At first, Robert's choice limited his teacher's capacity to generate the sense of community that he desired in order to make himself and his class genuine and productive. Schneider's choice to "love the big guy even more and all the way to the end" allowed several dialogues to emerge. A dialogue developed between Schneider and the incoherent "big guy" who was finally able to express a coherent idea, which in turn allowed the professor to address his class about the topic of the upcoming writing assignment. Then, Schneider and Robert were able to enter the breakthrough conversation in which the student shared the wisdom he had discovered about the new relationships he could have with his teacher, with his classmates, with himself, and with "people."

Developing Classroom Discipline
through Reciprocity

Some teachers fear that reciprocal relationships may lead to anarchy. They have seen schools and classrooms without discipline, and know that they are painful and unproductive not only for teachers, but for students as well. However, an educational environment that acknowledges the essentially reciprocal nature of relationships — among staff, among students, as well as between students and their teachers — produces not chaos, but order. And the teacher or administrator, because he or she occupies a position of authority, must make the first move to acknowledge the bond and create openings for all the stakeholders to establish authentic relationships.

That was the experience of Clara Dayag who, when she began her teaching career in a Los Angeles public high school, found colleagues demoralized by a lingering strike, overcrowded classrooms, unfocused students who openly used drugs and stole from one another, increasing numbers of students prone to drop out, particularly those without competency in English, and with limited resources. In the face of such chaos, she sought to reach out to her new colleagues, establishing relationships, channeling conversations to the positive, and trying not to judge her students by their prior behavior. She discovered, however, that she needed to be more proactive:

> I realized that in order to truly love these youth, I had to lay out clear boundaries of behavior. I reviewed the expectations, wrote letters and called home, followed through on the consequences and even gave F's to a few students. I worked doubly hard to make the lessons interesting and gave positive reinforcement to those making progress.

In San Antonio, Nancy Madison had a similar experience as she began her teaching career: "One of the first days I walked into the classroom, the students were all plastered against the window. Since I had been warned that they threw dictionaries out the window, I went over to see the situation. Instead, I found one of the boys being hung out the window by his heels. We were three flights up." She realized that she would have to show them the possibility of relationships other than the violent and antagonistic ones that filled that classroom, and sought to do so through persuasion, but without much effect.

Both Dayag and Madison made the first move toward establishing moral continuity in these impossible environments by recognizing the value of the least, and communicating that to the others. For Dayag, it was a ninth grader who came to class accompanied by his parole officer and wearing an ankle monitor. Although he countered with total apathy her attempts to engage him, the other students followed her every move as she tried to treat him with respect, allowing him space and time to try to become part of the class. Only during his last few days did he begin to respond with brief laughter, taking a few notes and doing some exercises. When he left the school because he had been given a new foster placement, he acknowledged his sense of having been accepted with a brief greeting before he left the classroom. She realized the impact of this relationship and others at the end of the year, when one of her students thanked her for how she "never yelled nor disrespected them, which showed that [she] was there truly just for them." The student also let her know that she had been looking on the Internet for a Bible study group because Dayag's "way of being in class gave her a hint that perhaps what made [her] strong was [her] faith."

For Madison, it was a sudden recognition that she had to "prefer" this most difficult of her classes because in them she recognized the countenance of Jesus Forsaken. She says, "From that point on it was a race to love Him — to say yes, and to make their suffering my own in the split second before any new outburst arose. I began to truly love that group. It was not that they showed any dent in their antagonism, but I found myself actually looking forward to that class because I was sure to find Him." After a particularly horrendous event, when a quarter of her class were removed because they had helped plan to set fire to the school, she explained to those who remained about the possibility of forming other kinds of relationships in the classroom, which could be summed up in one word — unity. She challenged them to take part in a deal to develop a cooperative, collaborative relationship with "whoever walked in the door," and asked those willing to try to sign an agreement. Intrigued, a few signed. As he left, one boy said, "I ain't never heard no teacher talk like this before. You're really strange."

In class next day, when the usual antagonistic behavior began, she made eye contact with the student, who had signed the paper, and in mid-sentence he stopped short. Other students noticed. The culminating experience came some time later when another teacher accused the students of stealing an object from her classroom. Her accusation created an uproar of defensiveness, and in response Madison told them, "If you say that you have not stolen the item, then I believe you," then suggested that they write the teacher who had accused them a letter stating that they had not stolen it, that they were sorry it had happened, and that they would like to help in some small way to contribute to its replacement. This suggestion provoked an outrage of self-defensiveness, and students began offering reasons why one of their classmates could not have done it. One boy's voice carried above the din, "Hey! Ms. Madison, is this what you meant by unity?" That one event did not create complete cohesiveness in the class, but it provided an opening to acknowledging and appreciating the value of reciprocity in their relationships.

At another time, Madison was teaching a "Basic Skills" class, a course with programmed instruction for students who could not handle regular instruction or who had previously failed a course. The classroom included two senior boys, for whom this was the last class they had to pass in order to graduate. Neither engaged himself in the activity of the class, yet they scored in the 90 percent range on tests. When she moved them to where she could scrutinize their work, their grades plummeted. She called attention to values such as integrity in the heroes of the stories they read in an attempt to help them accept the possibility of succeeding honestly, but one told her as he walked out, "What you're aiming at, Miss, ain't never gonna happen."

As with the disruptive class that she dreaded until realizing that she had to love them preferentially, she came to understand that she had "to see them with new eyes every day." As the term neared its end, she spoke with each of them separately. To the first, she said, "I don't have a lot to say, just this: in a few days, I'm going to be gone, so in the long run I don't matter at all. What does matter is that you'll be going home with yourself. You've got to live with your conscience, with whatever's between you and ..." She could see that her words made him uncomfortable, not because of the cheating, but because of the reality behind them. She went to the detention hall to have a similar conversation with the other.

Both young men had to pass the final exam to pass the course and so to graduate. They participated sullenly in the review sessions, but on the day of the exam made it clear to her that they had brought no materials with which to cheat. During the test, she could see that both were nervous and insecure, but worked diligently until time was up. She says, "They walked out without a word, but with an air of achieved dignity." Both earned minimal grades on the test, but passed. At graduation, the first of the young men stepped out of the line to get his diploma, walked over to her, bowed, and said, "Thank you." The other, whose success prompted the other graduates to a standing ovation, came to her smiling, the first time she'd ever seen him do that. He told her, "Thanks. I never thought I'd be that honest."

Although it is primarily teachers who can make the first move toward reciprocity in discipline, other stakeholders may find themselves in a position to do so as well. In suburban New Jersey, Teresa Scanlon took the initiative to do so when her eight-year-old daughter Diana was harassed on the school bus. She explains the situation: "A seventh-grade boy had made some racial remarks directed toward her on their ride home. When my daughter's friend got off the bus and left a vacant seat, the boy sat next to her and made insulting comments about African Americans. Making matters worse, other children also chimed in." Scanlon reacted with predictable outrage, and planned to contact the principal. She knew that such behavior would result in strong disciplinary action, which would be entirely justified. Nevertheless, she knew that punishment alone would not mend the rupture. "It seemed evident to all of us [she, the daughter who had been harassed, and her older daughter] that we had to embrace this suffering and live up to our commitment to live the gospel: we had to love even this boy."

The boy was made to apologize and was suspended for several days. Before his return to school, the principal asked Scanlon whether she and her daughter wanted to speak with the boy and his parents. Scanlon considered the possibility and realized that such a meeting would be useful not as a way of reinforcing the boy's punishment, but as a path to establishing reciprocity. She describes their decision in these terms:

This was my opportunity to start anew and to build a relationship with this family.

Diana and I prayed together and then decided to do three things at the meeting:

1. Show the boy love and forgiveness;

2. Educate the boy as to who Diana really is and where she comes from, because addressing the truth is also love;

3. Promise to become an example to the other children of how two kids who are expected to dislike each other (he had said nasty things, and she had gotten him in so much trouble) can still show each other kindness and prove they can go beyond the incident.

At the meeting, although the boy's mother was predictably suspicious, Scanlon resolved to not waver from the approach they had formulated. "I overheard her say under her breath that this would be trouble, and I really felt the challenge to live the plan we had agreed to." She, the boy, and his mother entered the principal's office and began their conversation. As Scanlon spoke, she "watched her expression change from embarrassment and defensiveness to acceptance. She was obviously surprised to hear this from the third-grade girl's mom. At the conclusion of the meeting, the boy shook my hand and promised to try to be an example."

Following this meeting, in response to what he had witnessed the principal wrote to Scanlon: "Thank you again for your gracious response and understanding of this incident and for those kind and uplifting words to the other family.... I was very touched by you ... please know that I am at your service and that I look forward to seeing you again under happier circumstances."

The boy fulfilled his promise, and the reconciliation that Scanlon and Diana sought came about. Later in the school year Diana was wearing a "Happy Birthday" pin, and her former tormentor made it a point to wish her well on her special day. She, in turn, shared with him some of the treats she had brought for her classmates. His punishment was certainly necessary, but what was essential — for him, for his mother, for Diana, for Scanlon, and for the school — was the re-establishment of a reciprocal relationship. Discipline may begin with rules and external sanctions for violating them, but is fulfilled through forgiveness, love, and acceptance.

TRANSFORMING THE ISOLATION OF SPECIAL-NEEDS STUDENTS

Schools place great emphasis on the value of individuality, yet that emphasis masks a subtle paradox. The individuality valued in classrooms must be constructed so as to conform to particular notions of order, reason, and self-expression. Those who for one reason or another cannot make themselves fit — perhaps due to having a particularly strong will, differing background from the prevailing culture, or physical or psychological difference — struggle to achieve those benefits of education that others seem to come by almost naturally. These kinds of learners are often deemed "special." Those closest to them, especially siblings or parents, often share in the burden of difference that impedes or blocks their entrance into the mutual dialogue through which authentic education is constituted.

Sometimes, as in the case of Brian Donovan, families suffer for years before coming to understand completely the nature of a child's inability to participate fully in school. His mother, Ursula, surmised that the scholastic difficulty he experienced from a very early age was due to his being among the youngest in his class. Even though Ursula sought to help him by tutoring him in the summer and enlisting the help of a relative who was a teacher, he continued to resist. By the fifth grade, he began acting out as the "class clown" in school, but at home collapsed in tears due to his anxiety. After that year, she and a team from his school that included his teacher, principal, resource teacher, and social worker determined that an individualized program would help him. Even though Ursula lamented his being kept from engaging in the normal interpersonal dynamics, she accepted the program and Brian became happier and more content to attend school. Ultimately, a teacher suggested that the family have Brian tested for Attention Deficit Disorder, and indeed a pediatrician found that his symptoms confirmed, at least in part, that diagnosis. The doctor did not prescribe medication, but with special tutoring, other resource help, and extra time Brian was able to complete high school.

Every adult in Brian's story — parents, teachers, principal, resource teachers, pediatrician — did his or her best to meet Brian's need to find a way to experience reciprocity during his school experience. Nevertheless, no one could relieve the burden of difference that prevented his entry into a dialogic relationship. The one closest to him, his mother, embraced the only strategy that suggested a path to resolution — to love Brian unconditionally, and to love those who sought to help him. She says, "I tried more often to make myself one with my son. I asked myself 'How would I feel if I was always at the bottom of the class, always struggling?' and I realized that I needed to help him willingly and to accept his limitations. Our relationship improved."

Brian has now completed his education, but remains unsure of the place he can occupy in the world outside school and family. Ursula reflects on his complicated life, and how it has affected both of them:

> Brian and I have a closer and improved relationship because I got involved and out of love tried my best to help him. I am becoming better at encouraging him and finding the right moment to say those words that he needs to hear. I know more about how the school

programs work and have met and become friendly with the resource teacher. And most importantly, I know that God is always there to send the right people to help and the right intuitions to aid me in my efforts to help my son become the child of God he is meant to be.

Frank and Louise Larsen had been trying to apply the Focolare spirituality of communion in their family life since early in their marriage. In making important decisions for themselves and their children, they considered their options in light of gospel values. They had been married for sixteen years when they adopted three-month-old Kevin from a Peruvian foster-care home. He had been weaned on a mixture of diluted formula and sugar water, and showed evidence of poor nutrition. He had delayed speech development, and seemed to have issues with comprehending and using language. The issues were compounded, perhaps, by the fact that Frank's job had taken the family to Geneva, Switzerland, where the family lived until Kevin was 10.

His family did all that they could to figure out how to help Kevin negotiate the school environment. Testing revealed expressive and receptive language disabilities, and he began working with a speech therapist and with a classroom aide. As he progressed from primary school tasks and relationships to the more complicated world of middle school, he began to resist more and more. One evening when the family was headed to a restaurant for dinner, his frustration and anger boiled over. He simply refused to go. Bit by bit, the story emerged of what had happened that day. He had been humiliated in front of the class because he had not read a book chapter that was years ahead of his ability. His teacher knew about Kevin's learning disabilities, but with 24 other students to contend with, it was difficult for him to keep in mind Kevin's difference from the other students.

Frank and Louise knew the long-term negative effects, both personal and social, of undiagnosed and untreated learning disabilities and knew that they needed to do all they could to love him and to understand what might be the best path to take. They also needed to discern how to deal with Kevin's issues as they related to their own needs, and those of their other three children. The family would have suffered had they stayed in Geneva and forced Kevin to continue on the current path, but they also would suffer if everyone was uprooted from their current location, where several of the family members were happy to remain. In the face of so many choices, when no single clear path presented itself, they turned to their grounding in the Focolare spirituality to understand not only what each of them might want, but what God wanted for their family. Frank comments, "What was most important to us was discerning the will of God. We knew if we did, that this would all somehow work out. We also had to do our part."

His employer offered to pay to send Kevin to an English boarding school, but they realized that dividing Kevin from the support of his family could not be what God wanted for him or for them. They researched other options, both in Europe and in the United States, and found a school in Minneapolis, their original home, which was a good match for his needs and abilities. After much prayer and discussion within the family, and with the full support of Frank's company, they moved back. Now, seven years later, his parents note, "He is not cured of his disabilities, but he graduated from high school as a healthy, happy young man with a positive belief in himself. We are now working to help him succeed in a college environment and discover a path in life where he can use his skills and talents. We have a tremendous peace inside that we really tried to understand what was the will of God for our family and what was the most love for Kevin."

Like Brian and Kevin, Lorenzo Taft has to live with a difference that impedes his easy integration into relationships. Unlike Brian, Lorenzo received a medical diagnosis early in his life. Knowing the name for his condition — autism — helped direct his family to resources and to experts where they found help for him, but such advice could not change Lorenzo's problematic way of dealing with the world. Like Ursula Donovan and the Larsen family, they came to understand that the ultimate help they could offer was unconditional love. His mother, Genevieve, writes: "We found out what really helped us to understand him and help him ... loving our son to the point of dying to ourselves, to our own way of thinking."

By entering into his experience, as Ursula did with Brian's and the Larsen's did with Kevin's, Genevieve and her husband Harold were able at least to appreciate the difficulty Lorenzo had to face in his day-to-day dealings in school. Also, as with the other families, the spirituality of communion suggested to them a way to accept him as he was. Genevieve explains:

> We could see him as Jesus Forsaken on the cross, especially when he was overwhelmed, confused, misunderstood, alone. Each time we embraced this Jesus Forsaken, accepting our son for what he is and simply loving him as he is, we found a special grace to help him and an opportunity for us to enrich our spirit. Our relationship as a couple became stronger and our daughter, living in this family atmosphere, gained a special maturity.

By embracing their son's suffering and recognizing its divine dimension, they found suffering transformed for Lorenzo, for themselves, and for their daughter. This embrace does not deny Lorenzo's needs nor can it "fix" his problem. It does, however, affirm his worth as a "child of God," a human being whose value does not depend on what he can do, but on who he is.

Genevieve notes that Lorenzo is sensitive to mood and tension in his environment; he feels comfortable and more social with people who are happy and accepting. He finds that environment in his family, but also in other groups of people who center their lives as they do around the Art of Loving.[1] In his English class, Lorenzo was asked to write a vignette about a community of his choice. He chose to describe a group of young people he met at the "Run for Unity," a collaborative sports event organized by "Youth for a United World," young people inspired by the spirituality of the Focolare Movement:

> What a pleasurable environment I'm in: playing games in the organization! Everyone is having fun,

---

1. See "Enhancing Reciprocity in a School Environment," p. 48.

CHAPTER 3

there is no rivalry, and the fun we have as we play is never wasted even if we lose. It's like I'm in the world of tomorrow already, a world with more joy, understanding, and unity.

Establishing and Maintaining Reciprocal and Dialogical Relationships through Home Schooling

Chiara Lubich noted that those inspired by a spirituality of communion wish to live "so everything is renewed: politics and art, school and religion, private life and entertainment. Everything" (*Essential Writings* 176). As is evident through the other eleven narratives in this chapter, most of those who strive to live the Focolare spirituality of communion do so in elementary, middle, and high schools, and in university settings, both private and public. The majority experience "school" in conventional educational structures. Some families who seek to live the Focolare spirituality choose to homeschool their children, as do a sizable number of others throughout the United States.[2] Catherine O'Leary notes in her experience below that many judge homeschoolers as reactionaries seeking to escape the real world. Their actual experience, however, is more complex. Homeschoolers can escape the institutional inertia that weighs down many educational reform movements, but they still must face problematic tensions between individual self-sufficiency and democratic relationships. This particular milieu within the "world" of education also can be renewed when suffused with a spirituality of communion, as shown through the experiences of the O'Leary, Jenkins, and Nyquist families.

External circumstances first led the O'Leary family to homeschooling. Because of Patrick's position as an army officer, they were living at a remote base in the Mojave Desert,

---

2. The most recent data from the National Center for Educational Statistics (2007) shows that 2.9% of the school-aged population in the United States are home-schooled (http://nces.ed.gov/pubs2009/2009030.pdf).

an hour's drive from the nearest town. Mark, a fourth grader at the base's elementary school, had a teacher with an alarming temperament. She would regularly tear up kids' papers in front of the class or humiliate them verbally with constant yelling and screaming. Catherine O'Leary notes, "We had two choices: either let him stay in the class, where his self-esteem and confidence and also education were in serious question; or homeschool him." O'Leary, who had been trained as a teacher, had serious reservations about homeschooling. "On our military base there was quite an extensive group of homeschoolers, and I had written them off as fanatics and isolationists." Nevertheless, her concerns about the teacher and the impossibility of finding another option led her to take this path despite these concerns.

At first, she tried to reproduce at home the experience of school — "lots of work sheets and papers and tests as proof that I was in fact giving my son an adequate education according to an outside standard set by the experts. It gave me security, but it didn't give my son a very exciting experience of learning." At that time, the O'Leary family had not yet met the Focolare; from the perspective of several years' experience in living its spirituality as a family, Catherine reflects on that early attempt at homeschooling:

> It really wasn't the way either Mark or I wanted to do things, but it was hard to have the courage to venture out. I had to face many of my own unfair and unrealistic expectations of perfection. I felt I had to produce a perfect genius kid, because it would prove all the naysayers wrong about homeschooling. At that point I was thinking more about me than what was the best for Mark.
>
> I also had to face the realization of my own weaknesses in both knowledge and character because with your own kids you have that "absolute power," so to speak, to be in control and make things just as we like them. I began to see that the line between offering a new and open-ended opportunity to learn versus becoming a dictator and grueling task master,

and pushing my kids to know everything, was much finer than I thought. I began to see more clearly that I had to choose between creating an environment focused on me and what *I* wanted for my children or one that would be more focused on Mark, how *he* learned, what he was interested in, where his talents were and what God wanted for him.

Mark's younger brother, Steven, recalls the effect on him and his siblings of his parents' choice of homeschooling as "the experiences and opportunities not just to love one another, but also to help play a role in each other's development." What made an even deeper impact on him, though, was the choice that his parents made and what it signified: "The risk taken by my parents in the way they took personal responsibility for our education has left an impression that has not gone, nor will ever go away." Writing from many years' perspective (he is now married and himself a military officer as was his father), Steven appreciates the academic and social benefits of homeschooling but, like his mother, sees the deepest value in the spiritual dimension of his education. "An unexpected consequence was the freedom that we had collectively, for my mother and father to choose how and what curriculum to teach us, and for us to be free to learn it in our own individual ways outside a classroom setting, enhancing the gifts God gave us."

A few years after they had begun homeschooling, the O'Learys met the Focolare Movement. They continued educating their three sons and their two daughters in this fashion as they lived in Germany, then in Muncie, Indiana, and in Louisville, Kentucky. When the two older boys reached high school age, they and their parents realized their need for broader social interaction and for the opportunity to join in competitive sports, so they enrolled them in the local public high school. O'Leary reflects on the educational journey she and her children had traversed, and the power of living a spirituality of communion to transform education by transforming relationships. She discovered that homeschooling presented many challenges, the most significant being maintaining moral integrity through loving, reciprocal relationships within that context:

There are many challenges to taking on the primary responsibilities of educating your own children — some from the state, some from pressures or judgments from family and friends, some from the children, but the biggest ones from ourselves. They come from what we realize about ourselves with regard to our need to grow in our ability to love consistently and without expectation. They come from the challenge of learning how to guide and direct and provide opportunities without applying pressure or negative methods of competition or judgment.

And these are the very same challenges that face all parents, whether they homeschool or not. They are there, but in the environment of homeschooling they can sometimes be more intense. For this reason I think it has the potential for stronger experiences that can be either positive or negative. With the light of unity and the love of the others that are also trying to live this way, those challenges can be met and be used as great tools.

The O'Learys began homeschooling out of necessity and later found their experience transformed by their lived experience of the Focolare's spirituality of communion. Gabriel and Kelly Jenkins, after exploring a variety of options, chose homeschooling at a certain point in their daughters' education because it fit the particular circumstances in which they were living and corresponded with their commitment to social justice.

When their girls reached school age, they enrolled them at the Early Childhood Center close to their home in Washington, D.C. Kelly explains their rationale: "This was our neighborhood, and it meant a lot to us to feel like we were sharing our time at the school and helping our kids to understand that they were part of this neighborhood." This setting presented a dilemma. They wanted their children to embrace real life in their urban environment; yet that meant exposing them to difficult or harsh realities, such as "infants and children left home unsupervised, boyfriends living with their moms, inferences about drug use, overtly sexual references that our children didn't understand, even things as simple as unhealthy eating habits." Gabriel and Kelly found ways of helping their daughters discover the positive opportunities within such experiences through the "Art of Loving" and sharing their love without the expectation that their friends would either feel the joy they felt, or find appropriate ways to love them in return.

When their older daughter turned five, she expressed the desire to attend the local parish kindergarten together with many of her peers. In many ways this proved a positive experience. Her teachers reported that she was always happy, and she did well academically. But Nellie herself found that the other children treated each other meanly and acted in antisocial ways, behavior that frustrated her because she saw no way to affect it positively. Gabriel and Kelly began exploring other possibilities, including homeschooling.

At first, they were not sure that it fit their notion of the egalitarian experience they wanted for their daughters. "To us, homeschooling seemed idyllic — sleeping in, taking vacation when we wanted, studying any subject we wanted. We weren't sure we could abdicate our public responsibility to the community and become part of a subculture without feeling morally guilty." They explored the homeschooling community in their city, the network of families who support each other's efforts through organized experiences such as trips to museums or through informal social meetings for parents and children. After doing so, they realized that homeschooling's real value lay in the freedom it would allow them to transcend boundaries of geography, race, religion, and politics. Moreover, they found that homeschoolers subscribed to values congruent with their own: "We would find as many friends of other races, denominations, or income levels in the homeschool community, but these friends would also be people who shared our belief that the human person needs to be at the center of any educational endeavor."

They have continued homeschooling since then. When they moved to a new city, however, they faced new challenges in finding ways of fulfilling the spiritual dimension of their educational vision. As Kelly puts it, "We were dismayed that there wasn't really a neighborhood that had the kind of diversity we were used to. We now live in a neighborhood where everyone around us is, statistically speaking, like us. Mostly Catholic. Mostly Caucasian. Mostly middle class." These circumstances made them work harder to fulfill their desire to live the gospel in their particular circumstances, to seek out what was presented to them so readily at the Early Childhood Center and in their former neighborhood. Kelly reflects on the value of the challenge that homeschooling in their new setting has required — not the struggle of coming up with suitable materials, teaching strategies, and schedules, but of building reciprocal relationships.

> This lesson has touched us deeply. Creating deep relationships requires work. I think that this may be the most important thing we have learned from homeschooling. To rattle off the statistical kinds of data that come to mind, our consistent group of "school" friends includes families with same-gender parents, families where parents are both working and homeschooling, families who attend or are faculty at the nearby Orthodox seminary, families of many religious affinities and of no religious affinity, families with one parent working at or attending a school, immigrant families, families in the more violent sections of our city, and families from the quaint towns just miles outside the city borders. Among all this diversity, we find a basic common thread: we all want to pay attention to the relationships among our families.

The Jenkins family chose homeschooling as the way that best suited their fundamental desire to change the world around them by living out the Focolare spirituality, which, as Kelly puts it, "invites us to love everyone and to make ourselves one with what is best in others." She reflects on the journey that they have been pursuing for the past eight years:

> That lingering question of whether we could have changed the world by leaving our children in a more institutional school setting is *almost* dissipated. We can see that they have affected children of many ages and the adults of our community. We can see that the

76

quality of the relationships they are able to develop with their teachers in homeschool environments have been reciprocal — each has gained from the attention of the other. And, we have become more certain that the fruits of these deep relationships are tangible and worth the work that is required of our family in order to develop them.

Homer and Martha Nyquist and their five children chose homeschooling within the larger call they felt to base all aspects of their family life, including education, on mutual love. Given that call, Martha writes that it is impossible for them to reflect on their experience except as an expression of a spirituality of communion. She acknowledges the distance between such a way of life and their actual lived experience as "being so very far from perfect" as well as the "many times when we didn't live mutual love while homeschooling (e.g., Mom losing her temper because she's worried we're not accomplishing enough, or losing her patience because a child wasn't learning his or her math)." Despite these all-too-human failures, she and her children see their choice of homeschooling as an expression of their living a spirituality of communion.

They identify some particular issues that homeschooling has allowed them to negotiate. The first is the choice of curriculum. Nyquist notes that the spirituality that suffuses their family and educational experience has guided their choice of materials and methods of instruction. They made choices based on values such as interdisciplinarity, dialogue, and awareness of their membership in the wider human family.

We looked for materials that would provide a view into other cultures, other parts of the world, other peoples — who are our brothers and sisters. One year we found a history, geography, and social studies curriculum that centered on major non-European cultures. Since our children were close in age, we studied that part of the world all together all year long, reading history and historical fiction, coloring pictures, dressing up and putting on plays, and doing all sorts of hands-on projects. Whenever possible, we tried to learn together, with all grade levels at the same time, from science to religion as well. We spent many hours all together in the living room, listening, while Mom or an older sibling read a great book aloud.

Homeschooling also let them discover ways of addressing pedagogical issues such as individualizing instruction, addressing different learning styles, engaging students' interest, the teacher's need for authentic authority and the students' need for authentic autonomy. As Nyquist reflects,

> Having so much time together gave everyone a chance to learn how to speak so others would understand them, to be patient with the younger ones' learning pace, to try a different way to show a concept — maybe with a picture, or even a song that could be memorized.
>
> The spirituality of communion helped to convince me that every one of my children was a unique creation and may not learn in the same way. So again, I tried to be flexible in choosing learning materials. Rather than, for example, insisting on rote memorization, I looked for something that would help to show the beauty of God's creation, the harmony of how numbers work together, etc. Rather than an authoritarian model, when possible, we discussed together what they might want to study next and selected materials together.

The sense of communion generated by their mutual interdisciplinary and multi-modal learning allowed them to address the difference in learning style of one of their sons. Joe's dyslexia was transformed from an obstacle to an opportunity for collaboration, self-sacrifice, and appreciation for another's struggle.

> Every one of us, from parents to older and younger siblings, has spent countless hours learning with Joe, reading his assignments to him, looking for ways to share information without actually doing the work for him, coming up with creative ways to remember

things, giving up time when we could have been relaxing in order to work with him.

The homeschool environment also allowed everyone in the family to acknowledge the value of investing extra effort in one particular individual. The brother to whom they donated so much time remains involved in their lives, and they see the positive effect on him and on themselves. "No one else in the family is as affable as Joe, as ready to smile, as ready to try and to work hard, and to lend a helping hand or listening ear when we need it." The Nyquist children have translated the lesson they learned from helping Joe to their experience as they take on educational challenges outside the homeschool.

We have always been in tune with our siblings' work load. Even with some in college now, we are always aware of the other's burdens; what assignments are due, what responsibilities we have. We know when the other is behind, and that they may need help in some other area so they can work on their school.

In any educational setting, teachers and students must find ways to deal effectively with the noisy distractions of popular culture that disrupt the inner peace and focus necessary for effective learning. Nyquist notes that "homeschooling made it possible to reduce, at least for a while, the cacophony of other inputs they could have received. With a little more space and quiet in our daily lives, they were able to discern more clearly the treasures of their relationships with others who were living the Focolare spirituality and with the church." As they enter their young adulthood, Nyquist notices the results of their years of focused education:

When they go into the world, every one of them is very much aware that they have something to offer. They have a lot of confidence that what they have to offer is just *so* good that they need to share it, and others will benefit from it. Their friends admire their welcoming openness to others, self-confidence, kindness, generosity, purity, and sense of purpose.

Like Catherine O'Leary and Kelly Jenkins, Martha Nyquist sees the power of homeschooling extend beyond the boundaries of the family to wider and wider circles of society. She reflects on the ultimate effect of their homeschooling experience in this fashion: "Our kids have learned to see each person as a gift, with a unique contribution. They are open to respectful dialogue with others on important issues, understanding that others are probably trying to follow their conscience as best they can."

BALANCING MORAL CONTINUITY
AND ACADEMIC REQUIREMENTS

The ethos of academic freedom in American schools, middle school all the way to college, gives teachers and professors the power to require material to which parents or students may object because of their sense of moral integrity. Such experiences can serve a salutary purpose, such as helping students recognize their unquestioned assumptions or prejudices. In the absence of a reciprocal relationship, however, they can compel students to value academic success and its rewards above the sense of morality and self-worth they have brought to the classroom.

When she was in the eighth grade at a large, progressive school district in the suburbs of Chicago, Rebecca brought home a note from her English teacher informing parents that the class would be viewing a film for the next three days. She downplayed the note as unimportant, but Rebecca is the third child in her family, and her mother, Carole, knew from experience that it would be important to review the film's content. When she did so, she found that although it contained some compelling themes, it also contained ideas, language, images, and actions with which she was uncomfortable, particularly for a mixed group of thirteen and fourteen-year-olds to view together.

It would have been simple to request that Rebecca be excluded from the class during the screening of the film, but that would leave other significant issues not addressed — Rebecca would feel discomfort at being excluded from something the rest of the class would be doing; but even more significantly, the film's objectionable material was inappropriate not only for their child, but for her peers as well.

Carole's first instinct was to write, as she described it, "an abrupt and legalistic" email to the teacher asking that the film not be shown. Such a message, however, would leave no space for mutuality. This event presented Carole with an opportunity for a deeper relationship with this teacher.

She decided to wait until her husband, Ted, got home so that together they could decide how to address the issue. They realized that this particular teacher as well as the school system as a whole had dealt with their children's needs well and wanted to affirm that, even as they objected to the choice of this particular film. They drafted this email message:

> We find neither solution suggested in your recent com-munication acceptable; neither the viewing of the film nor the exclusion of Rebecca from the class for the three class periods. What we do find acceptable would be the use of a non-objectionable, non-profane film which meets your curricular goals. We are sure you appreci-ate that having to sit out and do an alternative project creates a difficult situation for any adolescent and we certainly feel that your choice of film should not put any student in this embarrassing position. We ask that films be chosen with due sensitivity to the values of the families, so as not to place our children in an awkward position, also with their peers....
>
> We would not, though, want to complete this email without due regards to all the effort and time — heart and soul — that we know you put into the teaching of our children. Rebecca is our third child to have attended JHS and, like her brother and sister, flourishes in the professional, compassionate and stimulating environment. Enough thanks can never be given to you and the whole staff. The concerns we raise in this email in no way detract from all our appreciation. We just feel strongly on this issue and we feel confident we can work with you in finding an acceptable resolution to the problem.

Rebecca felt a bit of apprehension as she left for school the next morning but was at peace with her parents' intervention on her behalf. But even before school began, Carole received this email message in response:

Thank you for your thoughtful email. Instead of showing this film today, we will be showing [a different film]. I do want to be sensitive to all of my students' needs and values. I appreciate your kind letter.

As Carole and Ted had hoped, the response that they had crafted together transformed a moment of possible conflict into an occasion for mutual understanding and positive action. Carole comments, "As the year went on there were other moments to be in touch with her, not with problems but just other items, and we found her to be a real advocate and friend. The relationship was not just professional or distant, but more real." She adds that in addition to opening a more substantial channel of communication with the teacher, the experience also had a deep impact on Rebecca. "She saw that her values had importance and that it was safe to share them. In the relationship that developed between her teacher, herself, and her parents, Rebecca — all of us, surely — found a new sense of unity among us, as well as within."

Rachel, a college student of contemporary international literature, faced a similar dilemma when a required text contained graphic language and images that contradicted the gospel values around which she was seeking to order her life. When she sought to discuss her concerns with the professor, he met her discomfort with casual indifference. He suggested that she would get past the problem if she simply kept reading; her classmates, even though they also found the content of the book upsetting, told her to "just get through it," as dealing with such material was part of college life.

Roxanne, a Ph.D. student in dance, also faced such a conflict. The curriculum, which centered on dance and body politics, approached the topic through a post-Marxist, deconstructive theoretical lens. One particular professor claimed that critical theory should serve to make students question the value of religion or conventional notions like truth and beauty. The focus within his course on technology and sexuality included explicit and controversial material that made her feel squeamish, a discomfort compounded by her natural timidity and fear of receiving negative evaluations. She attempted to deal with her predicament by choosing topics with which she could feel comfortable yet fit within the purview of his critical framework, such as the social significance of precision dance performance like the Rockettes, or the value of 1960's social protest musical groups like "Up With People."

Rachel, unwilling to continue reading the objectionable text, told her professor that the book contradicted the way she lived her faith. In response he laughed, and assigned the class a quiz that he knew she would fail, as she had only read part of the book. Roxanne, having received no feedback from her professor, sought out her academic advisor, who urged her to remain in the program because she had much to offer the other students. Roxanne comments, "I didn't want to run away, but neither was I ready in any way to compromise my beliefs."

Although having to approach their situations from a student's relatively powerless position, both young women sought an opportunity for authentic dialogue through which to establish reciprocity with their professors. Rather than hand in a blank quiz, Rachel wrote, "I respect you as a professor and want to do my part and do well in this class, but I cannot read this book because I feel that it is destroying something I am trying to build within myself. I ask that you respect my views as I respect yours, and to offer me an alternate assignment." When she received her quiz back, he had written, "Okay, I understand. Do not worry about doing another assignment." As the course continued, for her semester project she sought his advice and found that her presentation became almost a direct collaboration with him. In a subsequent course with this professor, she found that he had included in the syllabus a section about mutual respect, which he requested that students show one another as he would for each of them as well.

On her way to a restaurant where the last class meeting would take place, Roxanne found herself in the same car with the professor and some other students. During that ride, he expressed interest in the topics she had chosen for research, suggesting that they were worthy of further investigation. Then he turned to her and asked her directly, "How is your spirituality going?" He had read her application file and was intrigued by her involvement with groups that sought to implement a collective spirituality in various social settings.

Students learn when they must re-evaluate the conventional wisdom of their unquestioned values and ways of making meaning, as do professors. Learning falters or dies when, through carelessness, arrogance, or intellectual and moral myopia, content supersedes the dialogic relationships through which education must transpire. Moral continuity can be balanced with academic requirements, whether professors take the initiative, or students.

REDEFINING EDUCATIONAL RELATIONSHIPS THROUGH RECIPROCITY

Contemporary notions concerning effective practice suggest that teachers relinquish their role as "sage on the stage" and take a more collaborative position as a "guide on the side." Such a call has, to be sure, a basis in the psychological processes that underlie the acquisition and construction of knowledge; but it gains a particular resonance in the context of a spirituality of communion. In a reciprocal environment, individuals acknowledge that they exist only if they exist in relationship. In a dialogic dynamic, the relationship between two (teacher and student, for example) actually includes not two, but three — each subject, plus the relation itself. Teachers like Jude Hoffmann, the subject of this narrative, seek a different perspective on classroom authority not only as a way of redistributing power so as to make learning more efficient, but out of love. In the context of a spirituality of communion, teachers and students who take the courageous step of setting aside their own ego out of love for another bring about a relationship that transcends their own human boundaries. During the first fifteen of Hoffman's more than fifty-year career teaching primary, secondary, and college students, he sought to avoid aspects of teaching that might provoke tension but relished his role as a mentor for minds seeking knowledge.

I never learned to like correcting my students' papers; that was always a form of penance for me. What I enjoyed most was being in a classroom with students, asking provocative questions, trying to get them to think about new ideas, answering their questions, and watching their eyes light up when they really understood something new. I worked hard to prepare these classroom experiences for my students and I suffered a lot when I was unable to prepare them well.

As much as the productive classes gratified him and his students, after coming to grasp with what a collective spirituality could bring to his experience, he found a new depth and value in teaching.

About thirty-five years ago I met the Focolare and I was inspired by the wisdom of Chiara Lubich, who was an extraordinary teacher. I started loving my students with more intensity, respecting them more and trying to see each one as a child of God. They often loved me back so that we could work in harmony together.

In this context, the value of effective educational practices became evident to him:

I even tried to correct their papers with love by taking care in my comments not only to point out their mistakes but to discover some good things to write even on the worst papers. I tried not only to be well prepared for every class, but to think up new and unusual ways of involving the students more actively in our discussions.

Establishing a classroom based on reciprocal relationships provides an opening for engaged learning, but does not guarantee success. The experience of failure, however, assumes a value and meaning that transcends the normal expectation of learning from things that do not turn out as expected. Hoffmann refers to a key understanding at which Lubich arrived: at the height of his suffering, when he cried out, "My God, My God, why have you forsaken me?" (Mt 27:46), Jesus Christ assumed all negative human experiences within himself. Therefore, every disappointment, every failure, becomes a presence of Jesus in his forsakenness, and therefore an experience not to be regretted or avoided, but one to be embraced and loved. Hoffmann recapitulates that understanding in this fashion:

> Every time I said "Yes" and put myself totally into his hands, I found that I had a bit of wisdom I never knew before. Chiara often said that Jesus is the teacher. This was most clear to me when I felt inadequate and empty. Then I felt closest to Jesus, to Jesus Forsaken within me. And as soon as I said, "Yes, it's you!" I received the light to understand that he teaches through his Holy Spirit, who gives us his gifts. That's how we too can be effective teachers.

Hoffman found the ideal of reciprocal relationships in educational settings was put to the test by the practical necessity of doing what he had once considered "penance" — evaluating student work. Without genuine reciprocity, grades can be construed by teachers and students alike as absolute justice or as deserved punishment for laziness, incompetence, or dishonesty. In a reciprocal relationship, however, evaluation becomes an aid to helping students achieve the critical self-examination they need for autonomy. Hoffman's insight into a spirituality of communion allowed him to live within the tension between his desire to maintain reciprocal relationships with his students, and his obligation to render judgment on the completeness or quality of their academic work. He notes:

> Although I do suffer with my failing students and am tempted to attribute part of their failure to my own inadequacies as a teacher, I have always believed that students' work has to be evaluated, as far as possible, for what it is. If I do not tell them the truth, then I fail to give them the dignity of being honest persons who resist fraud even when it is in their favor. If I want people to treat me honestly, then the Golden Rule requires me to do the same to them.

The divide between ideal and actual came into focus for him in one of his composition classes.

Arthur seemed to be the ideal student — affable, engaged, charming classmates and his professor alike. As the term progressed, however, it became clear that Arthur lacked commitment, skill, or perhaps both. Hoffmann notes, "He kept making the same mistakes over and over and getting the same low grades. In the end, he failed the course. It was painful for me to write the 'F' grade next to his name, because I really liked him. At the same time, I had to give him the dignity of being treated with honesty, because I really loved him as a son who needed to be told the truth."

He did not come to understand how Arthur interpreted this grade until a few years later, when Hoffmann was waiting in line to check out library books and heard a voice call out, "Hey, Professor, I never thanked you for failing me in freshman English." It was Arthur. Such a public proclamation is often meant ironically, but Arthur was serious. When he managed to talk to his former professor face-to-face, he said, "I'm not kidding. When I saw that 'F' grade, I was shocked, really shocked. You don't know how that turned my life around. I woke up and really started to study. I even became an English major like you! I always wanted to thank you. You told it like it is. That was just what I needed."

The relationship between Hoffmann and Arthur did not end there. A few years later, Arthur enrolled in Hoffmann's class in Milton's prose works, one the most demanding in the graduate curriculum. He announced, "Hi, Prof! Here I am back again to plague you." In this instance, however, his greeting was indeed intended to be ironic. He negotiated the class with great skill in composition and in discussion. Hoffmann considered the discussion he guided on "Areopagitica," one of Milton's most complex and demanding texts, "a mini-master class." It gave him much pleasure to assign "A" grades to this student, not out of pity or remorse, but because he had come by them honestly, just as he had honestly earned the "F" in composition.

This narrative took one more reciprocal turn. Some years after completing the Milton course, Arthur requested a letter of recommendation for a teaching position. Hoffmann surmised that part of the reason was the failing grade that still remained on Arthur's transcript. In a dialogical context, such an artifact does not remain a silent note of condemnation, but becomes an opening for reciprocity. As Hoffmann notes,

> In my letter to the school board, I said that Arthur proved to me in the graduate class that he really does have formidable teaching skills. He also demonstrated to me quite clearly in his response to the failure in the composition course that he has the personal experience that will help him understand what struggling students go through. I told them I would be surprised if he would not become one of their prize teachers.

FOSTERING AUTHENTIC COLLEGIALITY

The academic ideal is reflected in the etymology of the very word "college," the Latin *collegium*: "community," or "society." The actual relationships in institutions of higher learning, however, often fall short of that ideal. When Kathryn Pearson was hired by a Midwestern public university to create a graduate program in a new field alongside an established discipline, some faculty extended a welcome but a few of her new colleagues responded with emotions that ranged from "curiosity or indifference, to wariness, skepticism, or hostility." Similarly, in his mathematics department at a large urban university, Ryan Leahy found that divisions among some faculty reduced meetings to "screaming matches, with two distinct groups in constant opposition to one another." When he began teaching at a state university in the southeast, Edward Dennis "stepped into an environment that was very tense. It was not uncommon to hear threats of lawsuits. I remember one professor screaming down the hall. I saw faculty change directions as they walked across campus if they spotted one of their enemy colleagues approaching. The situation was so bleak that the provost declared a 'divorce' in the department." An entire culture cannot be extrapolated from these three anecdotes, but they do identify a tension within which university academics often must live.

Roger Nicholson's description of a "top-down" administrative model sums up one way in which this particular kind of tension manifests itself:

Relationships and dialogue between administrators and faculty are not valued. There is no sense of the interdependence of the roles played by administration and faculty for the greater good of the university. In this case administrators and faculty are isolated from one another and the university "community" is fragmented. A moral discontinuity can arise in this situation such that the good of the faculty, staff and students — indeed the university itself — is hurt by administrative decisions based on false or incomplete information.

The breakdown in relationships and dialogue and subsequent abandonment of a sense of interdependence occurs as well between individual colleagues, between factions, or within and between departments.

By living a spirituality of communion in such contexts, however, some university professors have found a way to live within the problem, and to transform the isolation that comes from strong personalities, professional rivalry, suspicion, and disciplinary boundaries. Nicholson describes such a spirituality and its application in an academic setting:

A spirituality of communion is based on the notion that humankind is one body with many members; and that the health and well-being of the body depends on the quality of the relationships between its parts. The quality of relationships is nurtured by dialogue where mutual understanding and respect are essential presuppositions.

As Pearson, Leahy, Dennis, and Nicholson have witnessed, the vacuum left by an absence of collegiality often fills itself with hostility or anger. Living one's spirituality in such a context cannot prevent such events, but does suggest a way of transforming oneself and in the process enlightening colleagues and even larger systems as well.

Pearson adopted a strategy which is central to a spirituality of communion, that of taking initiative even at personal cost — in the lexicon of the Focolare, "being the first to love." Coming into the university from outside and having the challenge of establishing a new program, compounded by the vigilance with which university departments protect their resources and power, she faced multiple challenges. In response to wariness, skepticism, or veiled hostility she tried to extend "concrete acts of love to establish the program within existing collegiality, inspired by the Focolare spirituality, strengthened by its community, and guided by the Holy Spirit." In establishing a core curriculum and organizing a teaching practicum for graduate students in her program, she chose to engage faculty from the department where the graduate program was housed, as well as from other departments and universities. "Doing so I knew would take more energy and time than working on my own and delivering my ideas to others. The Focolare spirituality, however, had taught me the importance of listening to others, valuing their ideas and cautions, and involving their help and guidance."

As she established her program, she faced many other points of contention, with her colleagues in existing departments as well as with teachers and students within her own discipline. In seeking ways to serve the university community or to help her own graduate students, Pearson applied the same approach of being the first to love. This love came to be expressed in many tangible activities: extracurricular lecture series and summer workshops; a program to mentor teaching assistants before they began their duties and through their first two semesters of experience; and creating a sense of community through welcome parties, celebrations when students achieved important milestones, reunions at professional conferences, and publishing a quarterly journal for the program's current students and graduates.

She has found that the climate she attempted to foster within the program at her own university "has permeated the goals of our entire field." Program directors in a consortium throughout the country meet to find ways of sharing courses, students, and resources. She notes that "an atmosphere of collegiality did not arise or sustain itself spontaneously. Our concrete acts of love in programs, classrooms, departments, and a discipline have contributed to this hundredfold, with the guidance of the Holy Spirit."

Edward Dennis looked for opportunities, however small, to find ways of bridging what seemed impassable divisions in his department. He sought to establish individual relationships where he could, sometimes being rebuffed and sometimes finding opportunities to build something more. The "divorce" that his provost predicted came about and his department split, each new unit offering a similar curriculum. The divide only complicated the problem, as there was considerable overlap between the two new programs; moreover, students were allowed to take courses only in one or the other, needlessly complicating their programs of study. He found an opportunity for concrete action when he learned that one member of the university's board of trustees worked in his field and was interested in merging various computer-related curricula. He prepared a Power Point presentation on how both programs could be realigned into distinct units within one school, so that students could take courses in both. After viewing the presentation, the trustee asked him why he was doing this. Dennis responded, "When a division seems irreconcilable, find a bridge." Some time later, a dean asked Dennis to head a new unit that the university was creating, comprised of the two formerly divided programs housed in a new school of communications and computer science.

Like Dennis, Ryan Leahy also sought to build bridges wherever possible. He describes his strategy for embracing the tension of disunity: "I have always known and believed that difficulties are best resolved by working collaboratively with others, and by building authentic relationships with them." He has no delusions about the difficulty of living in this fashion. "It is one thing to believe this, it is quite another thing to put it into practice especially when you feel that you are dealing with people who are antagonistic towards you and unreasonable. It is a delicate balance to live the virtue of justice, by giving recognition to those that deserve it, while at the same time trying not to slight the others."

His election as chair of his department has put his desire to live a spirituality of communion to the test. The provost had asked him, as part of the process of hiring two new faculty, to define the department's goals. He composed a memo, then realized that the critique of his proposal made by a younger, non-tenured professor was in fact superior to his approach and so circulated her ideas to the rest of the department, who embraced this new version. He realized the effectiveness of his ongoing efforts to unify the department when another colleague wrote to him about the importance of working collaboratively on this matter and the need to work in unity.

Not every experience produces such an obviously positive result. Although he tries to take almost every decision through consultation with the rest of the department, sometimes he must confront issues that resist a collegial approach. Because their program required a person with particular expertise, he once re-hired a faculty member despite the protests of the previous chair, who had let her go. On another occasion, he supported a secretary whom a colleague had accused of incompetence in order to cover up his own mistake. In situations like these, Leahy notes that his highest value is unity within the department, but that does not mean accepting or giving in to bullying.

In some cases, his administrative duties require him to take action that he would like to avoid, as when students lodged complaints about a lecturer whom he respected and trusted. He investigated the situation, found that the students' accusations were justified, and had to move to dismiss this teacher. In another instance, when he arrived at a retirement party, he found that some members of the faculty had been excluded, a division that reflected the long-standing antagonism within the department. In both of these cases, he sought a way to reconstitute unity. During the long process of terminating the incompetent faculty member, he sought to avoid antagonism with him, as well as with the union representative who was assisting in his case. A few weeks after the divisive retirement party, he hosted a gathering at his home for the entire faculty, now an annual tradition that he has continued as a way of bringing together people who had been in conflict. Leahy reflects upon his experience as a professor and as a chair:

> I have found that the Focolare spirituality has given me the strength but also the knowledge to handle difficult situations. The key is the Art of Loving, learning to make ourselves one, knowing how to set aside our own ideas, being the first to love, building unity with our neighbor and being able to live well the present moment. I do not bring problems home with me. Learning to live well the present moment allows me not to be weighed down with endless problems. By living my ideal of unity, by trying to love everyone and by being ready to transcend old hurts, much of the past antagonism has gone. Faculty meetings have once again become productive, and faculty members are beginning to work together and cooperate more, for the good of all.

Roger Nicholson had been asked by a colleague to create a program for developing proactive international projects in the wake of the September 11, 2001 attacks in New York and Washington, D.C. With the collaboration of a number of persons involved in peace-building efforts and interfaith dialogue, the program was launched. It drew upon the talents of professors from many different disciplines within the university, soon became financially self-sufficient, and under its guidance positive contacts and concrete projects were begun that paired universities in the United States with colleagues in Kyrgyzstan, Lebanon, Algeria, Tanzania, Uganda, the Philippines, Thailand, and throughout the Middle East.

After four years, however, the director of the interdisciplinary center under which the program was administered stepped down. He had approached his task from what Nicholson terms an "organic" model of leadership, in which he saw himself as a facilitator; he understood the term "university" as "a community of faculty, staff, students and administration all working together to carry out its mission for the benefit of all members of the community." It was congenial to work under the leadership of someone who valued dialogue and who fostered positive mutual relationships. The new director, however, operated from a "mechanical" leadership style which privileges keeping the "machine" of the university running smoothly, and which changes the parts of the machine if any risk is perceived. Such a risk surfaced after Nicholson had made a presentation about his program to a delegation that was visiting another college at the university. Some members of that delegation, whose first language was not English, misunderstood one of his statements and complained to the dean. Instead of investigating the complaint, the dean concluded that Nicholson's program posed a risk for the university and shared that impression with the interdisciplinary center's new director.

The director then denied the funds Nicholson had requested to hire an assistant, and noted that in his opinion the program was not interdisciplinary enough. He found the amount and number of new grants the program generated to be inadequate, and so had decided to transfer it from the interdisciplinary center where it had functioned successfully for the previous four years and to locate it instead in the department of Nicholson's home college.

Through the prism of a spirituality of communion, Nicholson reflects on this experience of unfair judgment and, in effect, a form of unjust retribution. In a sustained and eloquent commentary, he explains how key points of the Focolare spirituality have given him the clarity to discover God's love and support for him personally, even in painful and humiliating circumstances, and to not let disappointment and a sense of failure obscure the good that emerged even from his negative experience. Ultimately, through living a spirituality of communion in his academic context, he has come to grasp the deeper meaning of that experience and has come to see the positive consequences for his colleagues, for his students, and for his university.

> What happens when one is isolated from the power structure and lines of communication are not open? What do you do then?

In my case, I remembered the words of Cardinal Miloslav Vlk, then Archbishop of Prague, when he described the work of the Holy Spirit. He noted that today the world in which we live seems to be covered by "shadows" that often trouble or even overwhelm us. But if we allow the Holy Spirit to illuminate our hearts and minds and open our eyes, we can find points of light that give us hope and even joy. For me this meant to try to see where God was working in the activities of our program. It meant to focus on a pattern of providence in the work we were doing. It also meant that I had to take an internal step to embrace Jesus Forsaken. In this acceptance, I could find the love of God in the midst of the betrayal, hurt and humiliation and not lash out or seek revenge.

With this sense of God's love and support, I could return to my work with a more hopeful and even joyful attitude. I could focus on the positive relationships and outcomes of our work. I could focus on opening channels of dialogue and cooperation with my fellow colleagues and the associate dean now responsible for my program. This also meant to focus on the good we were doing around the world. I would often take time to look at the photographs of the faces of children in Kyrgyzstan or Algeria playing in our sports diplomacy programs. I would remember the happiness in the faces of the Muslim leaders who came to America being afraid of what they would find and going back home with a totally different and positive view of Americans and Muslims living in America.

In some ways, the pushback from some administrators in my university also reduced my ego and helped me remember that it is God, not me, who is achieving these results. My job is to stay united with the vine and to work closely and respectfully with the other branches both in the United States and in the countries in which we had projects. With this spiritual attitude, I felt we could better provide a caring and empowering communal atmosphere in the exchange programs that would touch the hearts and minds of our exchange participants. I must say that based on our survey results, we were very successful in this regard.

Besides this conversion of mind and heart, the focus on seeing the positive, and working in greater unity with others involved in the center, there were specific aspects of the Focolare spirituality that were very helpful as well. For example, "living the present moment" meant to move on after a difficult moment. It meant to work with what we have, not dwell on what we lost, or be angry over what could have been. It also meant "to put love where there is no love." That is, to love a Muslim guest who upon her arrival in the United States did not have any love for our country due to our foreign policies. At the end of her visit, she thanked me and said that she was happy to return home with the respect for America she had lost for some years.

Of course, the central aspect of a communitarian spirituality is the unity that comes from emptying oneself to be one with others … to share their joys and sorrows, to listen to their concerns and aspirations, and to take into consideration their ideas and points of view. When the possibility for unity was closed off in one direction, I learned to seek it in other directions. For example, when the director closed off the possibility for hiring an assistant to work with, I turned to my wife who was recently retired. We always tried to work together so that the projects were a reflection of that unity. In so doing, we drew into unity others involved in the center's projects in a way that contributed to the communal atmosphere enriched by a caring concern for our guests as well as each other. It was not uncommon for our exchange participants to say that they appreciated the degree of care we gave them, that it made them feel loved and secure far from home.

Finally, one aspect of the Focolare spirituality is "learning to lose" one's ideas for what in the end turns out to be the will of God. Though it was very difficult for me, the decision to transfer one of the program's key programs to another university worked out for the best. The university set up a team approach to running the program that makes it so robust that the team has been able to expand the program to a point where it can have nationwide impact through multi-year initiatives in developing countries. It now seems that the program will be able to achieve its potential for the good of our country and the world.

Strengthening the Identity of Religiously Affiliated Institutions in a Pluralistic Environment[3]

One of the challenges for religiously affiliated educational institutions is figuring out how to navigate between two poles that seem to be in constant tension: on one side, the institution's religious identity, and on the other, dialogue in a pluralistic culture. Those concerned about identity tend to focus on the issue of how to foster literacy in the tradition and transmit the religious identity to the next generation. Those concerned about dialogue, especially in pluralistic educational environments, tend to worry about the extent to which transmission of the religious traditions might alienate those who do not share the tradition.

In her contact with students at Fordham Law School, a Catholic Jesuit institution, Amy Uelmen realized what happens in students when these two dimensions do not cohere. She presented her legal ethics students with this problem:

You are a lawyer working for a law firm, only about six months on the job. Your supervisor, a partner in the firm, says there seems to be an ethics question about whether we can take this case, but it would be

---

3. A version of this narrative was previously published under the title "Sparks and Bridges: Catalysts of a Catholic Higher Education that Works," in *Current Issues in Catholic Higher Education* 26 (2007): 59–64.

very good for business if we could figure out a way around that. You do the research, and conclude that in your judgment there is indeed an insurmountable conflict of interest. What determines your approach to your research report to the partner — your own judgment, or what the partner wants?

About 85 percent of the class raised their hands: "what the partner wants."

The class reflected the general trajectory of graduate students who express little confidence in making judgment calls that implicate values, and who are paralyzed with fear at the thought of stepping off the beaten path. In class they work very hard to avoid discussions in which definitions of justice might conflict. Uelmen's primary concern was that even if they were "literate" in the Catholic or in any other religious tradition, it might not make a difference because they have not figured out how to connect their personal identity with their contribution to a work environment.

Or she observes an equally problematic swing in the other direction. Many graduate students believe that religiously grounded values systems create insurmountable conflict and should thus be avoided within the boundaries of public and professional life. In a class where Uelmen had presented the idea of "religious lawyering," one student rejected the idea outright, arguing that bringing religious values to bear on one's decisions necessarily leads to unacceptable bias, prejudice, and a kind of moralizing completely inappropriate for a professional setting. Uelmen pressed her: "So are you telling me that all lawyers must be cut from the same cookie cutter mold?" She answered, "Yes."

In this context, Uelmen realized that the task was not only to strengthen religious identity, or simply to navigate the challenges of pluralism, but that the core of the project was to link the two. Students need to see how a strong sense of Catholic identity, of being grounded in the tradition, does not necessarily generate entrenched polarization. And they need to experience how the openness of dialogue does not necessarily melt into vague and meaningless platitudes.

Grounded in the Focolare spirituality since her childhood, with extensive exposure to the Focolare's methods for fostering interreligious dialogue, Uelmen had already experienced in her own life and in Focolare activities how the dimensions of her own Catholic identity might correspond with a broad openness to the religious identity of people of other traditions. For this reason, she decided to map out her work as the director of Fordham's Institute on Religion, Law & Lawyer's Work along this dual trajectory. On the one hand, in her own scholarship, teaching, and in the programs that the study center sustained, strong, clear and unapologetic depth in her own Catholic tradition. On the other hand, she set out to build substantial bonds of friendship, openness and trust with her colleagues from other religious traditions. In her approach to the study center's programming, cooperating with a colleague who happened to be Jewish, she set out to create an open and respectful space for people to explore how their own non-Catholic religious traditions might serve as a resource for their approach to the law and legal practice.

What gradually emerged were two types of equally important "players," which they termed "sparks" and "bridges." "Sparks" are people who have the background and capacity to draw out the connections between their academic discipline and their faith, as well as the job security and sense of identity to actually accomplish it. "Bridges" are people who have the imagination and sensitivity to perceive how identity questions might sit with others from a different background or perspective. Intuiting what the concerns and fears might be, they are able to build relationships of trust that open the door to genuine communication about identity questions. In Uelmen's experience, both are essential, because real headway is made when sparks and bridges team up. The synergy tends to create a context in which principles of religious traditions come alive and become accessible, able to inform relationships and approaches to institutional conversations.

As a result of the dynamic, colleagues with whom she has been able to share something about the principles of the "Art of Loving" have felt not only free but also co-responsible for bringing a spirit of love to their interactions with students, other colleagues, and to their administrative duties. And Uelmen herself has been sustained by her colleagues' commitments and creativity. For example, one day a misunderstanding with another colleague had left her feeling slighted. Instead of attending a scheduled faculty function, she was tempted to remain by herself in her office. She was moping at her desk when a Jewish colleague called to ask, "Are you coming?"

"No, I don't feel like it."

He responded, "People are fragile. You have to love your neighbor. I'll save you a seat." What could she say to that? The event presented the opportunity not only to patch things up, but to find a deeper understanding with the colleague with whom she had the falling-out.

On another occasion she was at an administrative staff meeting seated next to another Jewish colleague who was also in on the agreement to find ways to let the principle of love permeate the school environment. At a certain point he leaned over and whispered, "We're not loving enough." This insight became the springboard for the two to work together with the administration to propose a creative solution for at least a part of the problem, and to offer help to implement the plan with a spirit of love and service.

The "sparks and bridges" synergy has also informed this little team's approach to faculty discussions about religious identity, in which over time about 25 percent of the faculty have participated. Uelmen has seen that the initiative and leadership of non-Catholic faculty has been essential for breaking down barriers of suspicion and fear. Each academic year begins with a "brainstorming" session to determine an annual focus. This approach from the ground up insures that the agenda is shaped by the faculty's actual interests, questions, and concerns, and that faculty members maintain control. This capacity to "let go" and leave space for everyone to express themselves has in turn generated profound openness to learning more about the Catholic tradition. Additional "sparks" and "bridges" have emerged. Several non-Catholic faculty members who have begun to discover the connections between Catholic values and what they are already doing would like to begin to integrate the tradition into their scholarship and teaching.

The "sparks and bridges" methodology has also helped to create a space to challenge students to grow. In her elective seminar, Catholic Social Thought and the Law, Uelmen challenges, the "sparks," those with a deeper sense of the tradition, to focus on how the principles play out in a pluralistic society, to keep an eye on how those tensions might change their perspective. She urges those concerned with the dilemmas of applying the principles in a pluralistic society to sit a little longer with the principles, to put on a "comparative law" hat so as to absorb and understand the principles, even if ultimately they may disagree with the framework.

Their encounters with each other in class discussions do allow them to catch a glimpse of what it means to move beyond the conviction or fear that the profession leaves room only for "what the partner wants," or for lawyers cut from the same "cookie-cutter mold."

Lubich's explanation of Jesus Forsaken on the cross, precisely in his capacity to empty himself out of love and as an expression of love, informs all of Uelmen's work. In her experience, this kind of love generates not a relativistic void but a creative space for the Holy Spirit to act and speak. This, she believes, is the source of light to understand how to preserve the religious identity of the institution, yet at the same time to appreciate the manifold ways in which God is already at work in students and colleagues of other religious traditions.

ESTABLISHING EDUCATIONAL INSTITUTIONS
THROUGH A SPIRITUALITY OF COMMUNION

From the perspective of a spirituality of communion, the highest goal of education is unity — within the individual, within the community, within academic disciplines, within human nature itself. Such fragmentation manifests itself in the tension between "the diaolgical, interactive foundations of the Deweyan vision of learning" (see p. 20) and the necessary emphasis upon the individual in the world of education. Enlightened theory and best practice can address such tension, but cannot resolve it. A spirituality of communion, however, offers a way to affirm the individual precisely through entering into reciprocal relationships, transforming the diverse experience of those involved in education into one of unity. In such a milieu, Chiara Lubich notes, "the spiritual and the human penetrate one another and become one…. Education's goal, its highest aim, becomes a reality" (*Essential Writings* 223).

The previous narratives have presented how individuals or small groups have worked within existing relationships and structures to transform division by establishing and maintaining relationships, by dialogue, and by reciprocal action. Those same strategies have been used by larger groups of people who have come together, led by a mutual desire to put the new commandment into practice, in order to generate enterprises devoted to the two goals Lubich identifies as fundamental to education: "to teach the individual and to build the community."

This narrative documents the experience of three entities that have been established in order to fulfill the goals of education in the light of a spirituality of communion — fostering the moral identity of individuals through reciprocal relationship and dialogue, and as a consequence building community. In the early 1990s, in response to Chiara Lubich's call for new initiatives that would promote a culture of giving, many educational institutions were founded throughout the world. Two are profiled here — Colegio Santa María di Actipan, in Acatzingo, Mexico (near Puebla) and the Café con Leche school, in Santo Domingo, the Dominican Republic. In 2008, the Focolare Movement opened the Sophia University Institute, a graduate level pontifical university devoted to inquiry concerning the implications of a spirituality of communion for philosophy, theology, and the social and physical sciences. It is located in Incisa Valdarno, near Florence, Italy. Each of these institutions is a composite of many individual and interconnected experiences, but they all share a common purpose: education within a culture of unity.

Members of the Focolare community organized Colegio Santa María to address the needs of their locality. Even now, more than a century after political independence, the indigenous people of Acatzingo de Hidalgo still bear the scars of colonial rule. Young people in the region exhibit elevated rates of dysfunctional family life, violence, depression, and suicide, reflected in poor academic achievement. The state school system is sparse, many girls abandon their studies after elementary school, and boys often enter the work force at ages as young as 11 or 12.

To address such a complicated and potentially hopeless situation, those who organized the school adopted two essential concepts. First, they told themselves, "We ourselves must be the 'change' that we want to see in the reality around us and in the world" (Medeiros 1). Second, they made a conscious choice "to not let ourselves be crushed by the reality, but to look it straight in the face, to love it and to transform it through remedies and practical solutions." In practice, they continue to strive for moral consistency between values and behavior, as well as intellectual consistency between understanding and experience. The school's director, Neide Medeiros, explains the basis for establishing such consistency:

> The theoretical strategies and educational praxis that we are developing are based on an important premise: the experience of mutual love among us must be real, must be *the relationship* that makes possible the living presence of Jesus the Teacher among those who form the educative community.

These essential concepts are played out in clear educational objectives. Medeiros outlines five of them:

- To motivate students to transcend the limitations of their personal, social, and cultural situations;

- To foster social awareness through which students and their families can overcome fragmentation;

- To develop logical, affective, and social skills;

- To tap students' emotional intelligence, that is, the "habit of entering into dialogue with the deepest and most intuitive part of oneself, of one's closest neighbors";

- To develop the capacity to make effective choices in one's actual experience of the world, and to reflect on the values which allow such choices. (2–3)

At a similar point in history, and for similar reasons, the Café con Leche school came to life in Santo Domingo, the Dominican Republic. Marisol Jiménez, a young woman active within the Focolare community, began to devote her free time to tutoring illiterate children in the impoverished Café neighborhood. In contrast to Colegio Santa María, which was founded upon essential educational objectives, Café con Leche has evolved by means of the volunteers through whose experience the school began. Over its eighteen years of existence, four characteristics have emerged:

- Solidarity. A key aspect of the Focolare spirituality is the "culture of giving." In the words of Margarita Rodríguez, one of the organizers, this means that "even though I am poor, there may be something that I can give to others that they do not have" (1). The school began through the efforts of volunteers who worked with families and children of the community, and is sustained today through the generosity of many within the Café neighborhood as well as sponsors and volunteers from the United States, Italy, Spain, and England. This culture of giving manifests itself in the school's many outreach activities: adult literacy classes, a community well, medical care, meals for students as well as for children not enrolled at the school, and micro-businesses for mothers and for young people. The students experience, Rodríguez explains, an "educational effect that is a fruit of the socialization to solidarity" (1).

- Fraternity. This is the sense of being members of one family among those who attend the school, as well as among their benefactors. At its inception, because Café con Leche was not recognized by the state and received no governmental support, children and families from other schools donated desks, instructional materials, food, and money. Rodríguez explains, "The children learned the dynamic that if something arrived it was 'providence.' We decided together who would benefit more from one thing, or who needed more of something else. We all sought the common good, as brothers and sisters of one family" (2). Volunteers from other countries have departed in tears because of their sense of leaving behind this "family." They had "come to know that what is really important is not only the help that they give, or service that they provide to a community, but rather that it is done out of love and is expressed concretely in the school community" (2). The same atmosphere touched the mayor, the supervisors from the ministry of education, even the president of the republic's wife. She had come to donate computers, and as it was her birthday the children sang to her. Moved to tears, she extended her fifteen-minute proforma visit to an hour. Months later she inquired from one of the school foundation's officers, "How is my little school?" (3).

- Reciprocity. The children realize that others have contributed to their school and that they too can participate in its support. At the very beginning, students kept piggy banks in which they deposited whatever they could save on its behalf. Now that the school is more solidly established, they "give back" through shared labor and service. With their parents, they work on the school's construction and maintenance. Graduates return to tutor younger children, and several have begun training to become teachers themselves. A lesson integral to Café con Leche is that sometimes one gives and at other times, one receives.

- Multiculturalism. Jiménez and her first students chose the name "Café con Leche," rich coffee swirled with milk, because they believed that their racial diversity was not a cause for division or a barrier to education, but an asset. The school today includes students from both the Dominican Republic and from Haiti, and the volunteers from other countries add to the mixture.

Each culture becomes a gift for the other, and the children —who rarely get the chance to travel — have broadened their mental horizons by sharing other countries' geography, history, stories, symbols, colors, songs, pictures, flags, foods and artifacts.

As mentioned in Chapter 2, since 2001 members of the Focolare's Abba School have held summer courses which conveyed to college students and recent graduates their method of intellectual inquiry as well as the content of their reflections. From these courses emerged the Sophia University Institute, a two-year graduate program in the foundations and perspectives of a culture of unity. Sophia enrolled its first cohort of students in October 2008. In his doctoral thesis, "The Focolare Educational Model at the Sophia Higher Learning Institute for Cultural Studies," Gianantonio Michelon describes the principal features of Sophia's method and content.

More than a school, Sophia is an academic laboratory in which faculty and students establish and maintain a community of life and thought through reciprocal dialogue. Building on the content of their previous academic studies in various disciplines, students construct new interdisciplinary, intercultural, relational skills. Michelon identifies four major themes in the learning outcomes of the Sophia Institute.

- Developing understanding and appreciation of cultural differences and acquiring relationship building skills through constructive dialogue and effective communication;

- Defining success as the completion of projects through teamwork and collaboration;

- Resolving interpersonal conflict through positive action;

- Connecting different areas of knowledge and their various methodologies. This is accomplished by analyzing complex problems and hypothesizing solutions by using multiple cultural resources. (8)

Like other institutions of higher learning, the Sophia Institute has a campus, faculty, courses, and students. It differs, however, in its strong emphasis on how each of these traditional academic components works at the service of building communion. The institute is situated in Loppiano, the first of the model towns established by the Focolare Movement to demonstrate the possibility of a community that includes people of diverse ethnicities, cultures, and faiths who allow themselves to be governed by only one "law," the commandment of Jesus to "Love one another as I have loved you." The life of the institute is grounded in this town's hallmark of unity in diversity. The faculty, all members of the Abba School, are committed to pursuing their teaching and scholarly agendas through a search for unity among disciplines, achieved not by eliding difference but by each emptying himself or herself so as to enter completely into the ideas of the other. Although each scholar teaches a specific discipline, such as theology, philosophy, social science, logic, or scientific reasoning, their courses are intended not only to convey academic content but to inculcate in students the culture of unity that the faculty have experienced through the Abba School. In its first full year, 50 students from 16 countries enrolled in the first cycle of the degree program.

Many universities gather large numbers of students from different nations and backgrounds. The uniqueness of Sophia, however, lies not only in the diversity of its participants, but in the gospel values that the faculty, students, and townspeople share. One student who attended a summer program offered by Abba School members sums up the effect of approaching study through a spirituality of communion:

> Sophia gave me a glimpse on how God could see unity in diversity…. We were able to come together and become a family and reciprocally enrich our lives. I saw and touched the reality of one big human family. The program spurred my intellect and deepened my faith, making me understand how faith and reason are reciprocal gifts to each other for the good of humanity.[4]

---

4. One draft of Michelon's dissertation included narrative examples from students and faculty he had interviewed. This appears on p. 168.

The fact that each of these three schools has grown and developed over many years suggests the usefulness and effectiveness of a spirituality of communion in the conception, implementation, and operation of educational institutions. The actual experiences of Colegio Santa María, Café con Leche, and the Sophia University Institute confirm the practicality of these models of education, as well as their impact on students, parents, staff, and the communities that they serve.

At Colegio Santa María, the faculty organize instruction around certain core principles. On the surface, these are typical of educational best practices. Students become aware that learning demands facing difficulty squarely. Lessons convey not only content but cognitive and meta-cognitive skills, effected through multi-modal, collaborative, constructive activities that convey to students, as Medeiros states, that "true understanding is grasped 'in relation' by deep and mutual listening and the possibility of displaying differing points of view. New elements come about, concepts are understood better, doubts are dispersed and explanations become clearer" (3). Students become aware of the affective and emotional components of learning, developing maturity within themselves and with their peers through dialogue, a capacity that they have learned through their teachers' passionate belief in the students' innate value, coupled with unconditional love and acceptance. The school creates a sense among students that the classroom is "their home, where they feel themselves free to act, to organize, and to share in the work of the principal and the teachers" (4). This is accomplished by fostering cooperation instead of competition, through service learning (older students tutor their younger schoolmates two to three hours each week), through alternative methods of evaluation in which single activities are used to measure growth across various disciplines, and by asking students to connect what they learn in school with what they experience at home and in their community. Medeiros describes how one of the high school students "took it upon himself to teach the adults of his village to read and write. He said, 'What I have learned here, I now want to give to others.' " Another helped establish a cooperative so that farmers in his community could experience the positive outcomes that come through collaborative instead of strictly individual action (5).

What students experience and learn at Colegio Santa María extends to deep levels that are apparent to the students, to their families, and to their community. At the end of the academic year, for example, the school bids farewell to graduates at a "Café Cultural," a celebration of song and poetry for those completing their bachillerato, who in turn share for their fellow students a synthesis of the meaning of their experience at the school. On the rigorous university admission exams, which only 30 percent pass statewide, 75 percent of Colegio Santa María students succeed; in regional competitions its graduates achieve the highest grades. This school, established to meet the needs of the most disadvantaged, attracts students from socially and economically privileged families as well, drawn not only by the potential for academic success, but also by the spirit of communion that suffuses the school. The state supervisor for public instruction, Pedro Hernandéz Andrade, was impressed by the students' sense of security, integrity, and academic success, but noted particularly the relationships he observed between teachers and students. He has proposed that the school be an educational model for all the schools in the State of Puebla.

Café con Leche, which began as a tutoring program for twenty-five children, has grown to a seven-classroom school that serves 600 students, their parents, and other members of the neighborhood. It has attracted a steady stream of international volunteers, drawn by the atmosphere of family and of love. Jessica Evans, a volunteer from the British agency i-to-i, wrote "All the children are so lovely, they are so happy all the time, despite having less than nothing.... I'm loving it so much, you can't leave without thinking about it all afternoon and evening. The kids never leave your mind."[5] Volunteers like Jessica in turn recruit others and through correspondence and fundraising maintain their connection to the school. Local volunteers have formed an NGO, "Fundación Foco"

5. See her posting on the "i-to-i" website, http://www.i-to-i.com/teach-english-in-the-caribbean-by-jessica-evans.html (14 September 2009).

(Foco Foundation, named after Igino "Foco" Giordani, one of the co-founders of the Focolare) to support construction and improvement of the school. Even though the school receives such private support, the local school district has agreed to fund quality improvement programs and pays staff salaries. As Margarita Rodríguez notes, "The local authorities have become increasingly sure that this is where the state's resources are best invested" (4).

Rodríguez points out other consequences of a school founded on principles and practices derived from a spirituality of communion. The Café community, as impoverished as it is, looks after the school's physical needs because they consider it not a separate institution but something they themselves own. The harmony of Café con Leche's clean, orderly physical plant gives witness to the possibility of beauty. Over the past seven years, there has never been an incidence of vandalism or theft, common occurrences in the district at large. Young people of the community serve as unpaid aides, seeing service as a higher value than the crime rampant in their lives. The students' behavior mirrors the physical harmony of the school. They respect their teachers and volunteers who work with them and accept each other as brothers and sisters. They rarely need to be reprimanded or drop out of school, and are sad as their education at Café con Leche comes to an end. Rodríguez sums up the school's educational outcomes in this fashion: "The core values [solidarity, fraternity, reciprocity, multiculturalism] made it possible for the school to build a strong culture that transcends what is usually found in the regular school system" (5).

In his study of the Sophia University Institute, Michelon identifies five "themes" that taken together sum up the experience of its students and their professors:

- The connection between Sophia and the Abba School;
- Interdisciplinarity as a hallmark of curriculum, instruction, and student life;
- Students' dual learning outcomes;
- "Trinitarian" interpersonal relationships;

- The effect of teaching and learning through a spirituality of communion.

Sophia and the Abba School: Sophia's educational model derives from the life and work of the Abba School. One student describes what the Abba School does, and how its experience is mirrored in Sophia:

> The Abba School grouped together ... scholars in different disciplines, around two goals: to study in an organic way, the meaning, and the weight of the different expressions of the Charism of Unity [that is, the Focolare spirituality of communion], and to examine what living the Spirituality provokes in the different disciplines, putting them in relationship one with the other. The experience of the Abba School ... that is, living the spirituality ... was very important.... This cultural experience was critical for the birth of Sophia University. (Michelon 114)

The students noted aspects of their experience that reflected those of the Abba School, qualities such as harmony, complementarity, and reciprocity. One of them summed up their experience at Sophia as being, "the first to love ... to be empty of oneself in order to listen to the other; it means to bring the other to create reciprocity, to make real this great experience of life within the Movement — and this counts also when we study" (113).

Interdisciplinary Curriculum, Instruction, and Student Life: Students follow a two-year course of study that includes theology, logic and scientific reasoning, philosophy, and the social sciences. The curriculum's interdisciplinarity emerges not by amalgamating discrete coursework into amorphous themes or units, but through the very notion of reciprocal relationships upon which Sophia is based. Amarylis Gott, from Colombia, turned down invitations to study at Stanford, Columbia, Georgetown, and Oxford in order to pursue the program at Sophia. This was, according to Gott, because Sophia had taken into consideration what I see as the most serious problems in contemporary society (such as individualism, poverty, injustice, joblessness) that have not been given a consistent answer. I thought that perhaps the answer is not to be found in those great centers of research and thought, but in a place where, in addition to study, every day is lived with people from the most varied backgrounds and cultures.... I have learned something more from these relationships with persons different from me. I have understood, during the classes, how many societal problems actually derive from the radical division between different ways of knowing among us as human beings. I could not have learned this in any other way.[6]

Even the daily rhythm of the university reveals its foundation in a spirituality of communion. As one student described the program, a typical day includes: "... moments of listening to and communicating about the Word of God, with Mass and the Eucharist at the center of the day, times for dialogue among the students and life in common, as well as moments of relaxation and sports, and ample time for research" (Michelon 134). In practice, these interdisciplinary relationships are reflected in the dynamic between professors and students, among professors, and among students.

One student defines the task of the professor as "a moment of welcoming that, as a consequence, creates [both] a relationship and [an opportunity for] constructive criticism" (136). They frequently use team teaching, organize classes around dialogue and set aside a one-hour block each day outside of class to continue it with students, and rely on student-led seminars. The professors, in turn, pursue all aspects of their professional work through the lens of relationship. One professor who had been teaching at the university level for thirty years before accepting a position at Sophia describes the way faculty members work together:

---

6. This statement is taken from a presentation that students made on 26 October 2009, at the beginning of the 2009–10 academic year at Sophia (authors' translation).

Everything is evaluated together: the project, the structure, the educational modules; but above all, your teaching is evaluated together.... I prepare my lessons and after that I check with my colleagues in two phases. In the phase of preparation I ask them if they like my outline, my points [of emphasis] ... therefore this is done together ... and then ... when I am teaching you have seven, eight, ten professors who are following what I am saying.... You have the awareness that your colleagues are listening to you.

Here, at Sophia, there is professionalism in doing things, there is professionalism and a willingness to let ourselves be involved together. (141)

Students, in turn, also work collaboratively to sustain and expand Sophia's interdisciplinary model, not only out of intellectual curiosity but out of a genuine desire to take the new commandment as the basis of their lives so as to merit the presence of Jesus among them (see Mt 18:20). Group study sessions extend classroom dialogue. One student describes such study in these terms: "It is a model of reciprocity, in listening to one another, and a gift — an exchange of their knowledge, of their requests, of their problems, of their doubts, and of their research. It is a very dynamic model of communication" (139). Given that these students have already completed a college degree in some area of specialization and that they come from different language and cultural backgrounds, finding common ground presents significant challenges. One student's experience reveals how these differences were negotiated: "I had a seminar on technology, and I introduced the theme of technology from the classical period up until modern times. Then for two hours, different reports were offered by engineering students, architects, and computer majors; but this inevitably touched social problems. Because technology is just one of the elements that define high tech society, it was useful to have a sociologist and a psychologist offer input" (140).

Learning Outcomes: Sophia brings about two principal results in the students: first, they sense that the program carries them forward in their search for wisdom, and second, they tend to develop an integrated sense of personhood. One student describes wisdom as "a light that allows one to understand knowledge in an integrated way" so that a "synthesis of wisdom" can be performed (115). The students describe their experience in this regard as finding a sense of personal identity to the degree that one "is in a relationship of reciprocity with the others," or having been formed through their educational experience to have "open minds that are able to dialogue and interact with each and every person" (117). In explaining the connection between the two goals, one student connects the development of knowledge with the development of the person:

> The educational goals converge. The first is to offer an integrated approach to knowledge (the different disciplines) in which the different disciplines combine to bring about a balanced global vision, of [the] human understood as a social being who in turn is part of the universe as a whole. The second one is to favor an integrated vision of the human person ... the psychological, spiritual, [and] the intellectual dimensions, with a strong accent on relationships. (117–18)

Through the content and method used at Sophia, faculty and students are able to discover unity of self as well as unity of knowledge. These outcomes touch students' personal and intellectual lives, but also include a spiritual component.

Trinitarian Relationships: In the recent encyclical *Caritas in Veritate,* Benedict XVI describes how the dynamic of personal relationships can be "illuminated in a striking way by the relationship of the Persons of the Trinity within the one divine Substance." The pope explains, "God desires to incorporate us into this reality of communion as well: 'that they may be one even as we are one' (Jn 17:22)." In this light, we understand that "true openness does not mean loss of individual identity but profound interpenetration" (54).

The faculty and students of Sophia see in the Trinitarian model not only great promise for the possible transformation of society, but also as a pattern for their daily educational interactions (118). In this light, the classroom can become an "anthropological," and even "transcendental" space in which the intellectual pursuit is fully harmonized with interpersonal relationships (123). A fundamental technique for fostering these relationships is "the pact," a reciprocal agreement among all involved parties to put into practice individually and collectively the new commandment of Jesus, "Love one another as I have loved you" (Jn 15:12). As one student described the effect: "From an intellectual standpoint, the pact has epistemic and academic consequences. Knowledge is shared and created as I get out of myself to give myself to the other, but also, the other is in this process and he enters into me" (126).

Teaching and Learning through a Spirituality of Communion: By means of four-week summer institutes beginning in 2001, and since October 2008 at its permanent campus, Sophia has expanded the scope of the Abba School's interdisciplinary, intercultural, relational work to an ever-widening group of students. The overall sense of satisfaction and happiness is reflected in one student's statement: "The experience leaves a sense of joy, of fullness, of discovery, where all the aspects of life are revitalized; so one has the will to do things, and [develops] trust. There are also other positive effects. It cures psychological wounds and offers all the elements proper to freedom in relationships" (143). Faculty found that the reciprocal relationships they were able to develop with colleagues as well as with students, the interdisciplinarity, and the multicultural nature of Sophia improved their effectiveness as teachers and enhanced their research within their own disciplines. One faculty member described his growth at Sophia as coming to a greater understanding of reciprocity and increased "trust in the educational relationship," whereby he came to perceive other faculty and students not as competitors, but as persons to be treated with respect (144).

Judith Povilus, provost at Sophia, sums up the shared experience of faculty and students:

The teachers convey their well-considered ideas, and new avenues open up as material for students' examination and inquiry. In this fashion, a culture is brought about that — as Chiara Lubich has affirmed — reflects the building of "new heavens and a new earth." She, in fact, insisted that experiences be concrete, connecting scholarship with its practical expressions in varied fields, such as economics, politics, art, "from which and in which will arise yet further scholarship."

And so begins again the dynamic process of dialogue between studies and life.[7]

---

7. Judith Povilus, "The Idea of a University in Chiara Lubich and the Sophia University Institute," unpublished address, 26 October 2009 (authors' translation).

Postscript

*I*n 1950, early in the history of the Focolare Movement, Chiara Lubich surveyed the state of the world and foresaw what she called "The Resurrection of Rome," the revitalization of every facet of human experience through the then-nascent spirituality of communion. She wrote, "Everything is renewed: politics and art, school and religion, private life and entertainment. Everything" (*Essential Writings* 176). Over time, her vision has begun to be realized through the experience of those who, touched by the charism of unity, have found ways of applying it in the circumstances of their lives.

The previous twelve narratives reveal how participants in various educational milieus have renewed themselves and the contexts in which they live and work. In one sense, the stories are quite ordinary. Each of these protagonists faces the same tensions as does any other student, teacher, parent, principal, or professor in the day-to-day experience of teaching and learning. But in another sense, they are extraordinary. By what Chiara Lubich has called the "divine alchemy" (*Essential Writings* 57) of the Art of Loving they have transformed division, distrust, difference, inadequacy, weakness, and failure.

This is not to suggest simplistic solutions to complex problems. Although each of these experiences proceeds in a few pages from an initial tension to a point of positive equilibrium, the actual paths contained many starts, stops, and re-restarts over weeks, months, and years. The "secret" to their resolution lies in a constant reorientation of self via practical application of a spirituality of communion, such as the Art of Loving. Even little children can do it, as with the Cube of Love. The narratives illustrate how applying simple principles produces results, some subtle and some striking. Individuals, families, small and large groups, even institutions are transformed through dialogue, reciprocity, interdependence, unity.

Although all of the experiences in this book developed out of overtly Christian motivations, a spirituality of communion does not presume a particular faith or conviction. It does demand, however, a sincere desire for genuine dialogue. Speaking at Westminster Hall, London (2004) on the possibility of a multiethnic, multicultural, multifaith society, Chiara Lubich described the prerequisites for such dialogue:

> Dialogue means that people meet together and even though they have different ideas, they speak with serenity and sincere love towards the other person in an effort to find some kind of agreement that can clarify misunderstandings, calm disputes, resolve conflicts, and even at times eliminate hatred. (*Essential Writings* 340)

Explaining the importance of the Golden Rule to an interreligious seminar at the Initiatives of Change Center in Caux, Switzerland (2003), she commented on the relationship necessary for "serenity and sincere love toward the other person":

> "Making yourself one" is not a tactic or an external way of behaving. It is not just an attitude of goodwill, openness and respect, or an absence of prejudice. It is all that, but it is something more. This practice of "making yourself one" requires that we empty the ideas from our mind, the affections from our heart, and everything from our will in order to identify with the other. (*Essential Writings* 347)

Entering into dialogue by making yourself one is not strictly Christian or even overtly religious. It is a way of engaging with others at a deep human level. It requires a willingness to set aside your own notions in order to enter the world of another, but — as these twelve narratives illustrate — what is gained far outweighs what is lost: the "something more" that Chiara Lubich describes is available to Christians, to those who profess other systems of belief, to any person of good will.

The next section contains documents in which Chiara Lubich presents the fundamentals of her vision of education in the context of a spirituality of communion. These include:

- "The Resurrection of Rome," a deeply mystical meditation on the spirituality of communion's effect on individuals and on society (1950);

- "Jesus the Teacher," an impassioned address to young people about the fundamental connection between Jesus in our midst and learning (1971);

- "The Charism of Unity and Education," an academic lecture at The Catholic University of America on her accepting an honorary doctorate in education (2000);

- A message to the participants at "The Community as Educator," the Focolare's first large-scale international conference on education (2006);

- "Children, Springtime of the Family and of Society: The Evangelization of Children," a colloquial talk to the Jubilee of Families at the Vatican (2000).

Appendix of Primary Sources

THE RESURRECTION OF ROME (1950)[1]

This passage, packed with dense, mystical imagery, is a meditation on the gulf between the Ideal world Lubich had seen during the period of enlightenment she and her first companions shared during the summer of 1949, and the gritty reality of the real world embodied in the city of Rome. The "resurrection" of Rome that she envisions begins by beginning to see the world and the people in it as God sees them, a vision that leads to a renewal of self, of relationships, of culture, of — as she puts it — "everything." It is a foundational document concerning the power of a spirituality of communion to renew social structures.

*I*f I look at this city of Rome as it is, my Ideal seems far away. It appears to me as distant as the days in which the saints and martyrs illuminated everything around them with that eternal light which reached even the walls of these monuments that still stand in witness of the love that united the first Christians.

In blatant contrast, today's world, with all its filth and vanities, dominates this city's streets and even more so the hidden recesses of every home where anger, every kind of sin and uneasiness lurk.

I would say my Ideal was a utopia if I did not think of Him, who also saw a world like this one. He was surrounded by it and at the end of his life appeared to be swept up by it, overcome by evil.

---

1. See Chiara Lubich, *Essential Writings* (Hyde Park, NY: New City Press, 2007), 173–78.

He too gazed upon the crowds around him whom he loved as himself, whom he created. He wanted to forge the bonds that would unite them to him, like children to a father, and unite them to one another as brothers and sisters.

He came down from heaven to reunite us as family: to make us all one.

He came with words filled with Fire and Truth that burned through the accumulation of vanities that cover the life of the Eternal that lives in every person and that passes among them. And yet, notwithstanding, people, many people, though understanding, did not want to understand and remained with lifeless eyes because their souls were in darkness.

And all this because he made them free.

He who descended from heaven to earth could have resurrected them all with a single glance. But, because they had been created in the image and likeness of God, he had to let them experience the joy of freely conquering heaven. Eternity was at stake. They would have the opportunity to live as children of God for all eternity, like God, creators of their own happiness (because participants in the omnipotence of God).

He looked at the world as I see it now, but he did not doubt.

Unsatisfied and sad as he watched everything going to ruin, he responded by praying at night to the heavens above and the heaven within, there where the Trinity lived, the true being, everything, while outside along the streets there was only emptiness that passes.

And I too follow his example so as never to separate myself from the Eternal, from the Uncreated, which is the root of creation and therefore the Life of all, in order to believe in the ultimate victory of Light over darkness.

I pass through Rome and I do not want to look at it. I look at the world within me and I cling to all that has being and value. I become completely one with the Trinity that lives in my soul, allowing myself to be enlightened by its eternal Light and filled with its heaven. I live in that heaven populated by the angels and saints who, not being constrained by the limits of time and space, can all convene in a unity of love with the Three in my humble being.

And I make contact with the Fire, that having invaded the depths of my humanity given to me by God, makes me another Christ, another God-Man by participation. Thus, my humanity merges with the divine and my eyes are no longer lifeless. Instead, through the pupil, which is the emptiness of my soul through which all the Light within me passes (if I let God live in me), I look at the world and everything in it. But it is no longer I; it is Christ in me who looks at the world and desires to make the blind see, the mute speak, and the crippled walk. They are those blinded to the vision of God living within them and outside them; mute to the Word of God that also speaks within them and that could be communicated in turn to others, reawakening the Truth in them. They are the crippled who are unable to move, because they ignore the divine will that from the depths of their hearts spurs them on to an eternal motion that is eternal Love, for when we transmit Fire we are set ablaze.

Therefore, opening my eyes once again to the world outside, I see humanity with the eyes of God who believes all things because he is Love.

I see and I discover my same Light in others, the true Reality of myself, my true self in them (perhaps hidden or secretly camouflaged out of shame). And, having found myself, I reunite myself to me, resurrecting myself in my brother or sister — because Love is Life.

Jesus is resurrected in them; another Christ, another God-Man, manifestation here on earth of the Father's goodness and the Eye of God on humanity.

Thus, I extend the Christ in me to my brother or sister and I form a living and complete cell of the Mystical Body of Christ: a living cell, a hearth of God that possesses Fire and Light, which must be communicated.

It is God who makes two persons one by placing himself third, as the relationship between them: Jesus among us.

Thus, love circulates and naturally carries with it (because of its innate law of communion), like a blazing river, all that the two possess to the point that all their material and spiritual goods are held in common.

All this gives concrete and outward witness to a love that is unitive, to true love, the love that comes from the Trinity.

Therefore, the complete Christ truly lives again in both persons, in each one and among us.

He, the God-Man, in the most varied human expressions imbued with the divine, placed at the service of the eternal design: God concerned with his kingdom, ruler of all, distributor of every good thing to all his children like a father who shows no preferences.

And I think that if I allow God to live in me and if I allow him to love himself in those around me, he would discover himself in many of them and many eyes would light up with his Light: a tangible sign that he reigns in them.

And his Fire, which destroys everything in the service of eternal Love, would spread like lightning throughout Rome resurrecting Christians and making this era, cold because atheistic, the era of Fire, the era of God.

But it is important that we have the courage not to waste too much time in other activities that simply reawaken a little Christianity, trying to echo past glories; or at least we should not give them the same priority.

We need to allow God to be reborn within us and keep him alive. We need to make him overflow onto others like torrents of Life and resurrect the dead.

And keep him alive among us by loving one another (and to love it is not necessary to make a lot of noise: love is dying to ourselves — and death is silence — and life in God — and God is the silence that speaks).

So everything is renewed: politics and art, school and religion, private life and entertainment. Everything.

The presence of God in us is not like a crucifix that hangs on the wall of a classroom as nothing more than a talisman. He is alive in us—if we let him live—as the legislator of every human and divine law, since he made them all. And from the most intimate recesses of our being he dictates them one by one. He, the eternal Teacher, teaches us what is eternal and what is passing and gives value to everything.

But only those who let Christ live in them, and therefore they themselves live in those around them, can understand this. Because life is love and if it does not circulate it does not live.

Jesus needs to be resurrected in the Eternal City and introduced everywhere. He is Life, the fullness of Life. He is not just a religious event....[2] This attempt to separate him from the entirety of our lives is a practical heresy of today's world. It subjects men and women to something that is beneath them and relegates God the Father far from his children.[3]

No, he is the Man, the perfect man, who sums up and contains all men and women and every truth and inspiration that they may feel in order to raise themselves to their proper place.

Therefore, the one who has found this man has found the solution to every problem, be it human or divine. It is enough to love him.

---

2. (*Note by Chiara Lubich*) It is sometimes thought that the gospel does not resolve all human problems and that it brings about the kingdom of God understood solely in a religious sense. But this is not so. Certainly it is not the historical Jesus or Jesus as Head of the Mystical Body who resolves all problems. This is done by Jesus-us, Jesus-me, Jesus-you.... It is Jesus in human beings, in each particular human being, when his grace is in them, who builds a bridge, opens the road. Jesus is the true, deepest personality of each individual. Every human being (every Christian), in fact, is more a child of God (=another Jesus) than a child of his or her own parents. It is as another Christ, member of his Mystical Body, that each person makes a specific and personal contribution in every field: science, art, politics.... It is the incarnation that continues, a full incarnation that involves all of the Jesuses of the Mystical Body of Christ.

3. (*Note by Chiara Lubich*) Humanity, in all of its human dimensions and capacities, is not to be mortified but elevated. Next to a renewed theology, "new" (because it is based on the trinitarian life lived in the Mystical Body of Christ) there also needs to be new science, new sociology, new art, new politics — new because they are of Christ, renewed by his Spirit. We need to set in motion a new humanism, where humanity is really at the center, that humanity which before all else is Christ and Christ in human beings.

Jesus the Teacher (1971)[4]

In this excerpt, Chiara Lubich speaks to young people concerning the Focolare educational method, which is rooted in the presence of Jesus in the midst. It is significant that she begins by speaking of Loppiano, the first of the Focolare's "model towns," which she describes as "a school." The English translation for *città*, "town," or "city," does not capture the Italian word's full connotation. *Città* refers not only to a physical location, but also to the life, laws, and relationships of the people who inhabit it. The function of Loppiano is to demonstrate the possibility of a *città* with only one law, that of the gospel, and therefore a place where Jesus himself, as he promised in Matthew 18:20, lives and works. "Jesus the Teacher" is not an honorific title or a theological abstraction, but a real person who conveys knowledge, wisdom, truth. As a school, Loppiano acknowledges what other teachers might provide, but first identifies the priorities for teaching and learning through a spirituality of communion.

Today I would like to tell you what I think of Loppiano, how I see Loppiano. It could be described in many different ways. But perhaps God has one particular role in mind for this little city: that of being a school....

However, while it is true that Loppiano is a school, that its role is that of a school, it is also true that it is a very specific and original kind of school.

In fact, the books, the classrooms, the courses, are not the primary elements that make it a school. No, Loppiano is a school because it has a Teacher. He is the one who inspired its founders on how this little city should be, how it could start out, how it should develop; he is also the one who lives among the inhabitants of this little city. We know that Jesus is the one who inspired this little city and who lives among its citizens.

Now, this reality is so great, so divine, that this school cannot be compared to any other. Which school has Jesus as its teacher? Not only, but if the teacher is Jesus, it means that his lessons must be very special and go far beyond any others,

---

4. Unpublished talk given in 1971.

even those of the greatest teachers on earth. Indeed, at times, it will seem that he teaches a knowledge that is foolishness to the eyes of men and women, even to the wisest. In other instances, it will seem that his is not even a doctrine, if by doctrine we intend a purely intellectual fact.

But one thing is certain: he who lives in our midst, in a little city like this one, is God and therefore he knows how to respond as a real teacher to all the questions posed by men and women of our times....

One milestone in our story is a period that dates back to the beginning of our Movement, when Jesus made us clearly understand that it was absurd to look elsewhere for the truth when he completely contained it; the Word, the Truth became a Person.

This period began when he practically said to us: leave the other teachers; follow me and you will learn everything. That was when it became clear, from the first things that he taught us, that there was a light which was not the fruit of reasoning but which came from above. It was then that he presented to us in contemporary terms the reality that St. Augustine felt so strongly: in the inner recesses of the soul dwells the truth. Then we ... gave a name to this light which came from heaven; we called it the "Ideal." It was then that God asked us to give up all the truths that others could share with us so that he alone could be our Master and teach us the truth. It was then that God gave us the strength to put all the books of other teachers in the attic so that he could reveal himself to us.

This moment in our history, with all its lights, is part of the foundation of all the doctrine of the Ideal. And it must necessarily be the foundation of whoever wishes to follow Jesus....

We are all called to put our books aside, at least spiritually, in order to understand in a true, vital and divine way the book par excellence, the book of God, the gospel, the Bible, which is the code of our new existence. It is not enough to do this just once. This decision must always be renewed in our hearts even when it is the will of God to study. Yes, Jesus wants us to cut with our own thoughts completely so that he may enlighten and clarify the truth for us, and help us understand how much truth others understood —famous scholars, for example, who history has not forgotten because they succeeded in capturing a ray of light from the Light of God himself.

This act of spiritually putting aside our books in order to know the truth is fundamental also for Loppiano as a school.

In fact, especially today, the world doesn't need cultured and learned people who have a lot of ideas. The world needs wise people filled with the Holy Spirit, who live the gospel, and of whom Jesus can say: "I thank you, Father, Lord of heaven and earth, because you have hidden these things from the wise and the intelligent and have revealed them to infants" (Mt 11:25)....

At this point someone might ask me: What has Jesus taught you in all these years? It's impossible to say it in a few words. The fact is that his light has been so abundant and so penetrating that it has reached the very ends of the earth. It continues to fascinate and attract countless people from every continent, ethnicity and culture. But if I should attempt to say a few words about what Jesus has taught me, has taught the Movement, I would have to say that he has given me a light that all the negative protests, all the heresies, all the straying from the truth, cannot possibly extinguish.

In fact, he said that everyone who listens to the Word of God and lives by it — and this is the point — is similar to a house built on a rock: the wind may blow, the rain may fall, the floods may come, but the house doesn't fall. What are the rains, the floods, if not the various doctrines more or less right, more or less balanced, that are the product of men and women's intellect throughout the centuries, that often fascinate and deceive people of our times with fleeting glimmers of light which then die out in order to make room for others?

Jesus, the Teacher, taught me that to understand the truth, to penetrate it deeply, to truly possess it, it is necessary not only to learn it well, perhaps to memorize it, but above all to put it into practice.

Very well, putting it into practice is a method of the gospel.

The Charism of Unity and Education (2000)[5]

This is an excerpt from an address given on the occasion of
an honorary doctorate degree at The Catholic University
of America, Washington, D.C. (10 November 2000). In it,
Lubich connects the theory and practice of education with
the cardinal points of a spirituality of communion.

As I have said on other occasions, our Movement can
also be viewed from a theological, philosophical, cultural,
social, economic or pedagogical perspective, as well as
from an ecumenical or inter-religious one. Let me share
with you now some of the ways that the more significant
points of this spirituality have had an impact in the area of
education.

In fact, our Movement and the various stages of its development can be viewed as one continuous, extraordinary educational event. All the necessary factors are present, including
an educational theory and a well-defined teaching method
that underlies our efforts to educate.

But first let us ask ourselves: what is education?
Education can be defined as the itinerary which a subject
(either singly or as a community) pursues with the help of
one or more educators, moving toward a goal considered
worthwhile both for the individual and for humanity.

What then are the characteristic elements of our educational
method, which emerge from the main points of the spirituality
we live?

Let us consider the first point: the "revelation" — if I may
use this term — of God as Love. We see that from the beginning of our Movement there has been only one *educator*, the
Educator par excellence: God who is love, God who is our
father. It was he who took the initiative. *With the intentional-
ity* characteristic of a true educator, he has accompanied us,
renewed us and given us new life along an intensely rich
itinerary of formation, both personal and communal.

---

5. See Chiara Lubich, *Essential Writings* (Hyde Park, NY: New City Press, 2007),
219–24.

He has enabled us and countless others to rediscover the true meaning of the greatest Fatherhood there is: a discovery of enormous importance, considering the various attempts in Western culture to affirm — on theoretical and practical levels — that "God is dead." There has been an eclipse of God's Fatherhood that has also contributed to an eclipse of the father figure, causing a loss of authority on the level of human and educational relationships. This has led to a moral relativism and an absence of rules in the life of the individual, as well as in interpersonal and social relationships. This often leads to grave consequences such as violence and the like, as if to agree with Dostoyevsky that "killing God is the most horrific form of suicide"... and "If God does not exist, then everything is permitted."

We have had the grace to come to know God. God is Love, and certainly not a distant judge, or a jealous enemy who uses his power to destroy us, or who does not take care of us. On the contrary, he is an educator who acknowledges each person's unique and distinctive identity, extolling the human being. He loves human beings, and this is why he is also demanding. As an authentic educator he demands and educates people in responsibility and commitment. God is love. For this reason he freed us from the greatest slavery of all, and re-opened the doors of his home to us. And we know the price his Son paid for our ransom. No educator has ever considered human beings as highly as a God who died for them. God who is love has raised each and every human person to the highest possible dignity: the dignity of being his child and heir. Each and every person!

It was precisely upon this understanding that we are all children of the same father that Comenius,[6] that great figure in modern educational theory, based his core idea: we must "teach everything to everyone."

Another key point of our spirituality is the Word of God.

"Teach everything to everyone." But in order to do so, one must use — as Comenius himself said — the educational

---

6. Comenius (1592–1670), an important figure in the Reformation, was from Moravia (in the present-day Czech Republic). Among his interests was education, and he attempted the first systematic understanding of pedagogy as a science.

APPENDIX OF PRIMARY SOURCES

principle of proceeding step by step. Thinking about it now, it seems that the Father suggested this method to us from the very first days of the Movement. He prompted us to live his word, choosing one sentence at a time from the gospel each month to be put it into practice in our daily lives.

But this immediately gave us "everything," because Jesus is present in his entirety in each word of the gospel (and when we live his word, he lives in us). At the same time, we were like children being nourished on his word and the more we were clothed in it, the more we grew into adults in faith and in life.

Through this very simple educational technique, which combines proceeding step by step with imparting knowledge in full, the light of this Ideal of life has spread and continues to spread far beyond the Movement as a powerful spiritual and educational experience that is constantly expanding.

The uniqueness of the word of God lies in its being *the word of life*, a word that becomes experience in a world that is frequently tarnished, even in education, by an abundance of empty words.

And we have experienced the power to educate, to offer alternatives, to challenge carried by this word, which is always alive and always new. Bit by bit, as it was impressed upon our lives, it gave them (and this is the tremendous task of education) an *existential unity*. This unity helped us overcome the fracturing and fragmentation that people often experience in relation to themselves, to others, to society, to God, while at the same time drawing out the originality, the unrepeatable uniqueness of each person.

Precisely because of this *existential unity* between word and life, between saying and doing, many people have found our experience credible and convincing. This experience provokes profound changes in people on an existential level, thereby setting in motion a true educational process.

The will of God is another point of our spirituality.

Faithfulness to the word of God also taught us to "put aside our base will," all those desires that still tie us to the narrow behavioral patterns of the self-centered "I." It helped us instead to follow the will of God, which leads us to transcend ourselves continually, in a movement beyond "I" to "you" that enriches us and makes us free.

As a rule, in the moral education of a person, one gradually moves from a necessary initial phase of dependency (*heteronomous morality*) to the *autonomous morality* that should characterize a mature adult subject. In our experience, too, we observe a movement from an initial adherence to the will of another and to his law (manifested in many ways) — which we grab on to like a *child* trusting completely in the guidance of an adult — to a powerful sense of freedom, the result of having made this Law *our own*. We then feel that it has become our law, that it has become so much a part of us that we feel *adult* precisely because we are able to say: "It is no longer I who live, but Christ who lives in me" (Gal 2:20).

And then another point: Jesus who cries out, "My God, my God, why have you forsaken me?" (Mt 27:46; Mk 15:34).

Jesus forsaken is our secret, our key idea, in education as well. He points to the "limit without limits" that should characterize our educational work, demonstrating the extent and intensity it must have.

But who is this Jesus forsaken whom we have decided to love in a preferential way? He is the figure of those who are ignorant (his ignorance is the most tragic, his question the most dramatic). He is the figure of all who are needy, or maladjusted, or disabled; of those who are unloved, neglected, or excluded. He personifies all those human and social situations, which more than any others cry out for education in a special way. Jesus forsaken is the paradigm of those who, lacking everything, need someone to give them everything and do everything for them. Therefore, he is the perfect example, the ultimate measure of the learning subject, who manifests the educator's responsibility. He indicates to us the "limit without limits" of the need for education, and at the same time, the "limit without limits" of our responsibility to help and to educate.

APPENDIX OF PRIMARY SOURCES

However, Jesus forsaken — who went beyond his own infinite suffering and prayed: "Father, into your hands I commend my spirit" (Lk 23:46) — also teaches us to see difficulties, obstacles, trials, hard work, error, failure and suffering as something that must be faced, loved and overcome. Generally we humans, whatever our field of endeavor, seek to avoid such experiences in every way possible. In the field of education, as well, there is often a tendency to be over-protective with young people, shielding them from all that is difficult, teaching them to view the road of life as smooth and comfortable. In reality, this leaves them extremely unprepared to face the inevitable trials of life. In particular, it fosters passivity and a reluctance to accept the responsibility for oneself, one's neighbor and society that every human being must assume.

For us, instead, precisely because of our choice of Jesus forsaken, every difficulty is to be faced and loved. And thus *educating to face difficulty* — which involves commitment on the part of both the educator and the one being educated — is another key idea of our educational method.

There are two other points that I would like to consider: unity and Jesus in our midst. In order to do so we should ask ourselves the following question: what is the aim of this educational process?

We share the same goal as Jesus. We could define it as his goal in educating: "May they all be one": therefore, unity — a profound, heartfelt unity, of all human beings with God and with one another.

Unity is a very timely aspiration. Despite the countless tensions present in our world today, the entire planet, almost paradoxically, is striving toward unity. Unity is a sign and a need of our times.

However, this drive toward unity within people — as the etymology of the word "education" (Latin *e-ducere:* "draw forth") indicates — must be drawn out in a positive way. This implies, on all levels of human endeavor, an educative process consistent with the demands of unity, so that our world will not become a Babel without a soul, but an experience of Emmaus, of God with us, capable of embracing the whole of humanity. This might seem a utopia. But every authentic educational approach includes a utopian thrust, that is, a guiding principle that stimulates people to build together a world which is not yet a reality, but ought to be. In this perspective, education can be viewed as a means for drawing nearer to this utopian goal.

In our approach to education, in which the spiritual and the human penetrate one another and become one (through the Incarnation), this Utopia is not a dream, nor an illusion, nor an unattainable goal. It is already present here among us, and we see its fruits when we live out Jesus' words: "Where two or three are gathered in my name, I am there among them" (Mt 18:20). Education's goal, its highest aim, becomes a reality.

In this we experience the fullness of God's life, which Jesus has given us, a Trinitarian relationship, the most authentic form of social relationship, in which a wonderful synthesis is achieved between the two goals of education: to teach the individual and to build the community. We believe that our experience of this Trinitarian, communitarian spirituality brings to fulfillment many ideas held by outstanding men and women throughout the history of education, whose initial premises were often different from ours, but who insisted on the importance of education in building a society founded on truly democratic relationships. One example among many would be the great contribution offered by John Dewey to education throughout the world, beginning with the United States. We also find many similarities in the recent concept of "service-learning," which affirms that the formation of the person should also involve a formation in and for the community.

Of course, our experience of community life is based on Jesus' invitation: "Love one another as I have loved you.... Be one" (see Jn 15:12; 17:21). This motivation is religious in nature, but it has extraordinary effects in the field of education.

The goal that has always been assigned to education (*to form the human person*, so as to render him or her independent) is implemented, almost paradoxically, by *forming the person-in-relationship*, which for us means *the human person in the image of the Trinity*, one who is capable of continually transcending self in the context of the presence of Jesus in our midst. It is through this spiritual and educational practice *of mutual love*, to the point of becoming completely one — a practice followed by all the members of the Movement, since all are called to live this communitarian experience in small groups — that we work toward the achievement of the *goal of all goals*, expressed in Jesus' prayer and testament: "May they all be one." As instruments under his guidance, we want to spend our lives for the fulfillment of this goal, which is at one and the same time a utopia, and a reality.

It is through this educational process that we as individuals and as community become capable of meeting with, entering into dialogue with, and working together with other persons, other Movements, and so on. And it is also through this in-depth educational process that, with God's grace, we can aspire to personal and communal sanctity.

Mary is an exceptional example of one who has put all the educational points I have mentioned into practice in her life.

Of course, Jesus is the one who fully lived out this pedagogical itinerary, in the dynamics of an experience that fully included both the life of the Trinity and his forsakenness on the cross. In his earthly experience, he lived interpersonal relationships with exceptional intensity, expressing empathy, acceptance and hope, and experiencing the struggle involved in educating, as well as a life of unity with the Father and with "his own." Clearly he is the most genuine and demanding witness of what it means to be an educator.

MESSAGE TO PARTICIPANTS AT "THE COMMUNITY AS EDUCATOR" CONFERENCE ON EDUCATION (2006)[7]

This message was sent to the first international convention for education professionals sponsored by "Education and Unity" (EDU — see page 41), held at the Focolare conference center in Castel Gandolfo, Italy. As in "Jesus the Teacher," Lubich emphasizes the notion of *città* (translated here as "community") as the context for education, a community made up of relationships. Such relationships, rooted in a spirituality of communion, renew not only the theory and practice of education, but society itself.

I am united to everyone — schoolteachers, post-secondary education teachers, representatives from ministries of education, experts in the field, university students and educators — who are gathered at Castel Gandolfo to participate in the international conference entitled "The Community as Educator." Since I am not able to be present, as I would have liked, I am sending all of you my warmest greetings.

"Our Movement and the various stages of its development — as I stated in 2000 while in Washington — can be viewed as one continuous, extraordinary educational event. All the necessary factors are present, including an educational theory and a well-defined teaching method that underlies our efforts to educate" (*Essential Writings* 219).

This is a firm belief that we can find right from the Movement's inception, when we referred to our initial experience together as a "School of Fire," in order to underscore the power of that Teacher who, present among us because of our mutual love, was forming those who later brought this new current of life throughout the world.

Thinking of education, in the gospel we find a sentence that can be of light for us: "You have one teacher, and you are all students" (Mt 23:8). For Jesus, then, there is only one teacher: himself. In stating this, he does not negate the existence of a teaching authority, but this needs to be un-

---

7. Unpublished address of March 31, 2006.

APPENDIX OF PRIMARY SOURCES

derstood not as dominion or power, but rather as service. In authority that is service, if it is love, it is not only the person who acts but really Christ himself in that person. In this way, Christ remains the only teacher.

Since we embarked on our adventure in this way of unity, we always sensed that we needed to learn from that sole Teacher. For this reason, in the many schools of formation that have risen up in our Movement, we always begin our lessons with a pact of mutual love through which the professors and students renew the proposal to love one another as Jesus has loved them. This is the necessary condition to merit his presence among them, as well as in each of them. And when this is lived out, they can hope to have him present as Teacher and educator.

This is the innovation of an education that is born from our spirituality of communion: educators and students find themselves relating as equals, as Jesus wants, as brothers and sisters in a Trinitarian relationship based on mutual love. The educators in this relationship are like the Father, while the students are like the Son. They therefore have to allow themselves "to be generated" — so to speak — by the educators, but also to love them. And they do this by trying to be "empty" of themselves so as to take in all that is transmitted to them; but also trying not to be timid and to share in turn what the Holy Spirit has helped them to understand. Also educators, on their end, have to try to be "empty" of themselves in order to welcome the students with their questions and contributions.

Experience has shown us that in such a climate of mutual love, the Teacher, Jesus in our midst, is light for everyone and guides us to an always fuller truth.

But such a relationship, based on this quality of love, must always be present also among educators. Only in this way will they rediscover their true mission and, by giving life to the Teacher among them — in their schools, in every educational environment — they will become builders of a new society.

It will be a society that will witness the emergence of a vibrant and strong fraternity in each of its cities, which will make them authentically open communities, with ideal conditions so that each person can express his or her own personality and fulfill their call in giving the best of themselves.

In asking Mary, who educated the Teacher, to share with us a bit of her maternal pedagogy, I wish that this conference may bring productive outcomes for all your work environments and your nations, for the whole world.

CHILDREN, SPRINGTIME OF THE FAMILY AND OF SOCIETY: THE EVANGELIZATION OF CHILDREN (2000)[8]

This talk was delivered at the Vatican on 12 October 2000 to the Jubilee of Families. Using children's and parents' own anecdotes, Lubich explains "a formation which is not only religious but fully human," particularly the Art of Loving and its practical application through the Cube of Love.

The gospels reveal to us Jesus' great love for children. St. Mark's Gospel says: "People were bringing little children to him in order that he might touch them; and the disciples spoke sternly to them" (Mk 10:13). And the evangelist Matthew: "When the chief priests and the scribes ... heard the children crying out in the temple, 'Hosanna to the Son of David,' they became angry and said to him, 'Do you hear what these are saying?' " (Mt 21:15–16).

In the face of the intolerance of the disciples and the indignation of the high priests, Jesus assumes another attitude. There is a real difference in the way he considers persons and events. He even holds up the child as a model of the disciple he has in mind. He says: "Unless you change and become like children, you will never enter the kingdom of heaven" (Mt 18:3).

Jesus' love for children is immediately reciprocated. They are fascinated by him. They are constantly beside him in his public life, and precisely because he loves them and is

---

8. See Living City Magazine, November 2004 (http://www.livingcitymagazine.com/content/2004/11/children-springtime-family-and-society).

loved in return, he becomes their friend and true "teacher." This was true not only two thousand years ago in the region of Palestine, but it continues to be true today and will always be true for the children of the world.

A mother recently wrote to me that her five-year-old daughter was torn between wanting to attend a meeting where she would learn about the gospel lifestyle, and leaving home for four days since the meeting would be held far away. It would have been her first time to stay overnight somewhere away from home. "One day," this mother wrote, "Angela came home determined. She had heard how other children were living the gospel. 'I want to do what they are doing. Let's get my suitcase,' she said to me, 'I'll bring shoes without laces and clothing without buttons, because you won't be there, Mom, to help me....' " These are experiences that make us smile, but it brought tears to the eyes of that mother, "because," she wrote, "I felt that Jesus had captured her heart."

"Education," intended as "a journey towards an objective" in the religious, moral, behavioral, cultural and social fields, is provided by different agents who often work in collaboration with one another. These are, first of all, the parents and the family, then nursery and elementary school teachers, the church community with its various environments and experts in formation, other informal groups, and the means of social communication.

Parents can effectively carry out their mission as educators by using to the best of their ability the special pedagogical resources of parenthood. These resources are enhanced by their personal experience and by the cultural legacy offered by their particular social context. This is the first and irreplaceable educational tool that by nature all parents possess.

However, there is also a wider and higher perspective. Christian parents believe that their child enters into the existential dimension as a "plan of immortality." Human life in God's plan begins weak and helpless, then grows and develops through interaction with other persons and with creation, and finally overcomes death and enters into the everlasting newness of heaven, becoming and living as a "child of God." Such was the human journey of Christ. In order to carry it out, he needed to be "welcomed and helped to grow by a simple and poor family," as John Paul II said; "simple and poor," yes, but surely in possession of those spiritual and human resources which made it a suitable environment for the formation of such a Man.[9]

Each family must believe in the love of God, who not only gives the gift of life but also prepares for each of his children the environment in which to grow and the way to follow. But what is the way? We know it: "I am the way," affirmed Jesus himself. "No one comes to the Father except through me" (Jn 14:6). Ultimately, to educate a child means to help him or her encounter Jesus.

The sentence "Let the little children come to me ..." (Mk 10:14) is a sublime synthesis of the gospel's method of education towards a formation which is not only religious but fully human.

Could it be that it was easier to meet Jesus two thousand years ago? I'm not sure. The history of salvation goes on and Christ continues to be with us, as he promised. He promised to be present in different ways and these are points of contact between himself and the family.

One way Jesus is present is found in that well-known and explicit declaration of his: "For where two or three are gathered in my name, I am there among them" (Mt 18:20). Therefore, he is present where people are united, which means, according to many Fathers of the Church and the traditional interpretation of the Catholic Church, being united in him, in his will, that is, in mutual love which is his commandment. Now, can a family, can a couple fulfill that condition for which, according to Origen, Christ is "attracted and called"[10] to be present among them?

Everyone recognizes that the family is already an interaction of love, of human love which links the father to the mother; the two of them to their children; the children to

---

9. John Paul II, Angelus, *L'Osservatore Romano*, 26 December 1999.

10. Origen, *Commentary on the Canticle*, 41, p. 13, 94B.

APPENDIX OF PRIMARY SOURCES

their parents, the children among themselves and then with aunts, uncles and grandparents and then the aunts, uncles and grandparents with nieces, nephews and grandchildren. Now if the family also draws from the divine love offered by Christian life — that divine love infused in their hearts by the Holy Spirit — then Christ can truly be in their midst, rendering effective the grace of the sacrament of matrimony.

Parents who love one another in this way bring Jesus into their home.

How can we describe this human-divine love, this "gospel love"? In practice, how can we love as Jesus wants us to love?

We must really focus our attention and try to understand what we could call Christ's "Art of Loving." It is demanding. It requires us to *love everyone*, to *take the initiative in loving*, to *love always*, to enter into the reality of the other person, *making oneself one* with the other person, and to see and love Jesus *in the other, in any other person*, according to his words, "... you did it to me" (Mt 25:40).

If husband and wife love one another and love others in this way, always starting over, knowing how to die to themselves out of love for the other, their mutual love, which brings Jesus the Teacher into the home, attracts the children.

Children naturally tend to imitate the behavior of their parents. If this is so, considering the family only from a human viewpoint, what could happen when the parents are bearers of the grace of the sacrament and the mystical presence of Jesus himself among them?

I have the good fortune to receive many letters from children, because the youth sector of our Movement also includes the very young; and I notice the spontaneous educative action of a family that seeks to live out this love based on the gospel.

Betty, a six-year-old, wrote to me, "Sometimes I talk with Jesus. The other day I was in my room doing my homework and I began to talk with him. I told him many things and I didn't want to stop talking to him. You know, when I make an act of love, I feel something beautiful inside, like someone who pays me a compliment and who says 'thank you' to me. I think it's Jesus."

And a French mother wrote to me, "Before putting my children to bed, I kneel down with the older ones. Last night, Catherine pointed out to me that David, the youngest, kept on playing. 'Let him be,' I said, 'it's his way of praying.' So we recollected ourselves to say our evening prayers. When we opened our eyes again, David was beside me with his hands joined. 'You see,' said Catherine, 'if we love, Jesus teaches him, too.' "

With regard to our spiritual experience we can say, as we often repeat, that we were "born with the gospel in our hands," and we keep going like this. We choose one sentence at a time and we put it into practice in our daily lives for a month. In this way our life becomes "evangelized" and immersed in God, who is *completely* present in his word.

With this very simple pedagogical technique of gradualness and fullness, God led us to a strong educative and spiritual experience, one that is in continual expansion. It is an experience which involves our families, too, and the families of the communities that gather around the Focolare houses and share our spiritual journey.

In these families, just as they prepare the food so that little children can digest it, so too must they give the gospel in a way that can be understood by them. We adults in the Focolare take one sentence every month, with a commentary approved by the Church that is easily understood, and we try to live it out during the small and big events of the day, in a holy and joyful competition of love with the children. If in the evening, mom and dad share episodes of how they were able to live as Christians on that day, the children will naturally do the same and tell their own experiences of putting the gospel into practice. These are moments in which responsibility and reciprocity wonderfully weave together family relationships.

Children who grow up in families like these are naturally formed day after day in a mentality that is in conformity with the gospel, which will lead them to view persons and situations as Jesus would, in line with his way of thinking.

They will learn to see humanity as the large family of the children of God, to use the things of this world with a pure heart and a spirit of solidarity. They will have a proper hierarchy of values which will always guide them in life.

Of course, they, too, will have their trials and periods of crises and searching. Especially as adolescents and in the early years of their youth, we will have to deal with their rejection and protests, but no attitude, however serious, should block or turn off our love for them. The Art of Loving that Jesus taught us will indicate the way to understand them deeply in every way possible during the various stages of their growth. It will put on our lips the right word of advice; it will always keep us open to dialogue and to sharing their interests. We will learn to even "waste time" with them and succeed in making them our friends and winning their confidence.

But even if the rejection persists, we will always keep the door of our home open, and we will recognize in our suffering a trace of the suffering of Christ crucified who also lived the abandonment on the part of everyone, even on the part of the Father. And we will accept it as he did, remaining serene.

We know, however — and many confirm this — that all the values instilled in our children will remain because in the most important moment of their lives, when the foundations of one's personality and character are laid, they had the good fortune of encountering Jesus, present in the midst of their parents and present in their lives through his word.

In 1998 I had the idea of proposing a game to them: to write on the sides of a cube the rules of the Art of Loving, which I spoke of before. I invited them to roll the cube in the morning when they woke up and to choose how they would love everyone they met that day. There was an incredibly enthusiastic response from children and adults all over the world.

One father wrote to me, "I was washing the dishes when Luke came into the kitchen. He took a dishtowel and began to dry the dishes. 'Be careful, don't drop them,' I said, a little surprised by his generosity. With a sense of satisfaction, Luke replied, 'When Mom comes home, she'll find everything clean. You know, Dad, when I go to heaven, Jesus will say to me: that time you helped your Dad, you helped me.' "

We have thousands of people in need whom we help in a special way, and the children contribute. Mark wrote to me referring to the fact that some parents tell their children, "When you lose one of your baby teeth, put it under your pillow and the tooth fairy will come and leave you some money." And so he wrote to me, "Dear Chiara, Mommy and Daddy told me that you have been looking at your accounts to find money to help people. I'm sending you the money that the tooth fairy left me for the first tooth that fell out. You know, Chiara, I did some calculating: I have eleven more teeth that will fall out, so … Chiara, I'm sure we'll make it, and then we won't have any more poor people in the world!"

May Mary, who raised a child who became *the* teacher, bestow on us at least some of her skills.

Works Cited

Fondi, Enzo, and Michele Zanzucchi. *Un Popolo Nato dal Vangelo: Chiara Lubich e i Focolari*, trans. Amelia Uelmen. Milan, Italy: San Paolo, 2003.

Geertz, Clifford. *The Interpretation of Cultures: Selected Essays*. New York: Basic Books, 1973.

Gilligan, Carol. *In a Different Voice*. Cambridge: Harvard University Press, 1982.

Groome, Thomas. *Educating for Life: A Spiritual Vision for Every Teacher and Parent*. New York: The Crossroad Publishing Company, 2001.

Hauerwas, Stanley. "Constancy and Forgiveness: The Novel as a School for Virtue." *Notre Dame English Journal* 15, No. 3 (Summer 1983) 23-54.

Lubich, Chiara. *A New Way: The Spirituality of Unity*. Hyde Park, NY: New City Press, 2006.

———. *Essential Writings: Spirituality, Dialogue, Culture*. Hyde Park, NY: New City Press, 2007.

Lubich, Chiara, et. al. *An Introduction to the ABBA School: Conversations from the Focolare's Interdisciplinary Study Center*. Hyde Park, NY: New City Press, 2002.

MacIntyre, Alisdair. *After Virtue: A Study in Moral Theory*. Notre Dame, Ind.: University of Notre Dame Press, 1984.

Medeiros, Neide. "Metodi e Metodo" [Methods and Method], trans. Thomas Masters. Address, "Community as Educator," Castelgandolfo, Italy, 31 March 2006.

Michelon, Giannantonio. "The Focolare Educational Model at the Sophia Higher Learning Institute for Cultural Studies." Ph.D. diss., University of the Incarnate Word, 2009.

Orrill, Robert, ed. *Education and Democracy: Reimagining Liberal Learning in America*. New York: The College Board, 1997.

Rodríguez,Margarita. "Presentación de la Escuela Café con Leche: Como se traducen los valores de la espiritualidad del focolar en el campo de la educación." [Presentation of Café con Leche ("Coffee with Milk") School: How the Values of the Focolare Spirituality are Translated into the Field of Education], trans. Stephen Schubert. Unpublished document.

Taylor, Charles. "The Dialogical Self." In D.R. Hiley, J.F. Behman, R. Shusterman, eds. *The Interpretive Turn*. Ithaca, NY: Cornell University Press, 1992, 304-14.

_____. *Sources of the Self: The Making of Modern Identity*. Cambridge, MA: Harvard University Press, 1989.

Walker, Margaret Urban. "Moral Understanding: Alternative 'Epistemology' for a Feminist Ethics." In E.B. Cole and S. Coultrap-McQuin, eds. *Explorations in Feminist Ethics*. Bloomington, IN: Indiana University Press, 1992, 165-175.

Authors' Information

Michael James earned his bachelor's degree in Theology and Psychology from the University of Notre Dame and a Ph.D. in Educational Policy Studies from Indiana University, Bloomington, IN. James also held a number of administrative, teaching and research positions at the University of Notre Dame and Indiana University. He was the senior student affairs and enrollment management officer at Mount Marty College, South Dakota before serving as Vice President for the Association of Catholic Colleges and Universities in Washington, DC. James is currently a Fellow in the Center for Catholic Education at Boston College where he directs the Institute for Administrators in Catholic Higher Education, teaches in the Higher Education program graduate concentration in Catholic University Leadership, conducts research and lectures on Catholic university leadership and mission, and is a co-editor of the journal, *Catholic Education*. James also serves on the boards of Ministering Together and the Conference for Mercy Higher Education.

Thomas M. Masters holds a bachelor's degree in English and Philosophy from Lewis University, a master's in English Literature from DePaul University, and a Ph.D. in Language, Literacy, and Rhetoric from the University of Illinois Chicago. He has taught English at the Leyden High Schools, Franklin Park, IL; humanities at Lewis University; rhetoric and composition at the University of Illinois Urbana and at the University of Illinois Chicago; and in DePaul University's Multicultural Urban Educator program. He has lectured and published widely concerning the history of writing pedagogy and has worked with a variety of educational reform initiatives through the Focolare Movement's Education and Unity. He is editorial director for New City Press.

Amy J. Uelmen holds a bachelor's degree in American Studies and a J.D. from Georgetown University, and an M.A. in Theology from Fordham University. She currently serves as the director of the Institute on Religion, Law & Lawyer's Work at Fordham Law School where she teaches and writes in the area of Catholic social thought and the law. She has lectured and published widely on how religious values might inform the practice of law and how principles of dialogue might inform debates about religion in the public square. She is a frequent contributor to the Focolare Movement's monthly magazine, *Living City*.

Notes

Notes

Notes

Notes